Hostile Ground

Hostile Ground

Defusing
and
Restraining
Violent
Behavior
and
Physical
Assaults

Edward Lewis

Paladin Press • Boulder, Colorado

Hostile Ground:
Defusing and Restraining Violent Behavior
and Physical Assaults
by Edward Lewis

Copyright © 2000 by Edward Lewis

ISBN 1-58160-054-2
Printed in the United States of America

Published by Paladin Press, a division of
Paladin Enterprises, Inc.
Gunbarrel Tech Center
7077 Winchester Circle
Boulder, Colorado 80301 USA
+1.303.443.7250

Direct inquiries and/or orders to the above address.

Visit our Web site at www.paladin-press.com

TABLE OF CONTENTS

CHAPTER 1: INTRODUCTION TO CONFRONTATION 1
Fear
Transforming Fear into Power
Physical Danger vs. the Emotion of Fear
Personal Power and Body Language
Eye Contact
Restraining and Protecting
General Tips

CHAPTER 2: THE AGGRESSOR 9
The Verbal Aggressor
The Physical Aggressor
Other Types

CHAPTER 3: BODY LANGUAGE 13
Signs of Stress and Deception
Signs of Impending Violence
Your Body Language

CHAPTER 4: ASPECTS OF ASSAULTIVE BEHAVIOR 21
     Phases of Assaultive Behavior
     Assaultive Behavior by Age Group
     Basic Communication Model of Assaultive Behavior
     Environmental Conditions
     Model of Basic Needs and Reasons
     Response Procedure

CHAPTER 5: DEFUSING A HOSTILE SITUATION 29
     Getting the Subject's Attention
     Finding His Motivation
     Building Rapport
     Preliminary Strategy
     Interview Defusing Techniques
     Intervention Defusing Techniques
     Show of Force
     The "We" Attitude
     Outside Resources
     Negotiation and Other Strategies

CHAPTER 6: RESTRAINING AND MANAGING PHYSICAL ASSAULTS . . 39
     When to Restrain
     The Professional Restraining Team
     Restraining Holds
     Law Enforcement Restraint Techniques
     Parole/Probation Situations
     Public Servants
     Civilians: The S.A.F.E. System
     Attracting Attention and Using the Environment

CHAPTER 7: LEGAL ISSUES 85
     Use of Force
     Arrest
     Revised Code of Washington (RCW)

CHAPTER 8: DEBRIEFING 113
    Injuries
    Analysis, Notification, and Follow Up

CHAPTER 9: REAL-LIFE STORIES 117
    Mental Health: Quiet Time to Violence
    Mental Health: Fearful Patient
    Mental Health: Laughing Turns Violent
    Child Protection: Struck with Screwdriver
    Private Investigation: Surrounded by Bouncers
    Private Investigation: Interview Suspects of a Burglary Ring
    Private Investigation: Surveillance and the .357 Magnum
    Community Corrections Officer:
        Arresting Subject in CCO's Office
    Community Corrections Officer: Arresting Subject at Home
    Self-Defense Situation: Road Rage
    Transit Bus Operator: Gang Trouble on the Bus

REFERENCES 133

ACKNOWLEDGMENTS

I would like to dedicate this book to my parents, Carey Lewis Sr. and Felicidad Lewis, for their guidance, patience, and encouragement to succeed. This book is also dedicated to my children, Alex and Mike Lewis. Hopefully they will see that if they think positive and try hard, they too can succeed.

I would like to thank the following individuals for assisting me with this book:

Carey Lewis Jr., my brother, contributed to all aspects of this book. His experience working in correctional institutions, child protective services, and a mentally ill offenders unit provided valuable input.

His son, Carey Lewis III, with 20 years of martial arts experience (taught by his father with 30 years' experience), contributed to the self-defense section.

A special thank you to SWAT officer Don Gulla for providing me with law enforcement scenarios for dealing with hostile situations and physical aspects of restraining as taught at the Criminal Justice Training Center in Seattle, Washington.

Another special thank you to Darryl Briggs, a transit bus operator for 18 years, music producer for Dajari Productions, and martial artist. Briggs provided defusing techniques used by transit drivers and real-life stories.

Registered counselor and private investigator Janet Harris provided input on observing mentally ill subjects and investigations.

Private investigator Mel Hoover of Hoover Investigations contributed real-life stories.

Robert Detamore provided me with scenarios and tactics used by community corrections officers.

A special thank you to our photographer, Glen Grover, who devoted a lot of man hours to this project. The following people served as photo models in this book: friends and former students of Yao Mun Nomad Martial Arts Glen Grover, Julie Grover, Don Gulla, Paul Osness, Ross Barde, and Lee Leggore; my brother Carey Lewis Jr. and nephew Carey Lewis III; my partner in private investigations, Janet Harris; and law enforcement officers Gary Drake, Jeff Barden, and Tim McClung.

I would like to thank the Washington Association of Legal Investigators (WALI) and Linda Montgomery. This association of private investigators has provided continuing professional education for me. The ethics, professionalism, and morals that they display are honorable and well worth emulating.

Most of all, I would like to give my Glory and Honor to God, the Father Almighty.

PREFACE

*In a confrontation, as long as the subject is "talking" and not
"doing," then there is no true danger. There is only true emotion.*

Edward Lewis

Hostile Ground was written for professionals who must deal
with people who often exhibit assaultive behavior, including the
mentally ill, the irrational, and criminal elements of society.
Mental health workers, social service personnel, self-defense
instructors, security guards, public servants, process servers, private
investigators, correctional officers, and law enforcement officers can
learn a lot from this book. It will provide these professionals with
methods to defuse or, if necessary, restrain an attack from a subject.

While reading this book, please note that certain tactics and
techniques may be applicable only to specific circumstances or
occupations. For example, mental health professionals may have the
option to retreat and call in an on-site physical-restraint response
team, whereas a police officer trying to defuse a violent person in a
shopping mall may have to deal with the situation with or without

backup. Likewise, a civilian may be legally justified to defend himself with lethal force under certain circumstances, but a person working in a public-service position may be under professional or legal constraints precluding such a response. Overall, however, the general principles of defusing and restraining assaultive behavior outlined in this book are applicable to most situations.

Hostile Ground does not claim to present any legal or moral advice. Laws vary from state to state, and you must be familiar with these laws before engaging in any confrontational situation. If you are not familiar with the pertinent laws in your jurisdiction, consult the proper agency or an attorney before using or applying any of the information contained in this book.

The author, publisher, and all other persons associated with the production and distribution of this text specifically disclaim any and all liability, loss, and risk, both personal or otherwise, that may be incurred as a consequence, personal or otherwise, directly or indirectly, of the use or application of any of the information contained in this text.

Please keep in mind that, in order to avoid awkward phrasing, I have chosen to use the masculine identifier when describing either a subject or a professional.

CHAPTER 1

INTRODUCTION TO CONFRONTATION

Most confrontations begin with a verbal or mental battle. Sometimes they end with a physical assault. When all else fails, people often resort to a physical form of expression.

During a verbal confrontation, many people feel uneasy. This could be due to a lack of confidence, fear of physical violence, or the inability to defuse a hostile situation. If, however, you learn to read the telltale signs of aggression, learn techniques to defuse the situation, learn how to physically manage an assaultive person if necessary, learn to recognize a truly dangerous situation, know the laws pertaining to use of force, and understand what is true danger and fear, you will develop confidence. This will allow you to be more calm and controlled during a confrontation so that the chances of the situation reaching violence will decrease.

FEAR

Fear is a feeling of disquiet or alarm caused by an awareness or expectation of danger. Fear is *not* a negative feeling—it is a natural one. For one to be comfortable with fear, one must understand its strengths and weaknesses.

Because we do not experience fear as often as we do our relaxed, everyday demeanor, we become uncomfortable when we experience it. We often interpret this as lacking confidence, not being in control, or not being strong or brave.

The internal feelings a person experiences during fear are actually *positive* changes in his system that prepare him with extra mental, physical, and spiritual energy. More blood, adrenaline, and oxygen flows through the body to add extra energy and strength. Erratic thinking is simply the spirit and brain trying to coordinate, much like an electrical meter that monitors whether power transmitted into the system is being used.

Fear is only natural. Don't be ashamed of it. It has probably saved your life before and will do so again.

TRANSFORMING FEAR INTO POWER

You can transform fear into power and strength by changing the way you perceive fear. First, you must believe that the effects of fear on the body are, in fact, your system's way of helping you defend yourself. This can be done through meditation, positive thinking, or prayer. Surround yourself with people who believe that this transformation can take place. Convince yourself of this fact.

Second, you must understand where your fears come from within you. When a confrontation intensifies through increasingly aggressive voice and body language, fear creeps in: you are wondering what will happen next, and it is this "unknown" which you fear. Once you know how to identify the unknown and learn how to deal with it, you can control fear, and it now can be transformed into power and confidence.

PHYSICAL DANGER VS. THE EMOTION OF FEAR

Usually before a physical encounter takes place there is a verbal confrontation. There is no physical danger during this stage because the confrontation is only between minds, emotions, and spirits, not bodies. True physical danger comes only when two or more people come in contact with the intention of committing bodily harm to each other.

Fear generally is felt before and after rather than during an encounter. During a physical engagement, you will be doing everything possible to defend yourself and restrain the attacker; there will be no time to feel fear.

Before the situation turns physical, however, you will be thinking of what to do and the potential consequences. After the encounter you will think about what mistakes were made, how to correct those mistakes, and what lessons you learned. During these two thought processes, emotions will be running high, your adrenaline will be pumping, and sometimes shock will set in.

Remember, as long as you keep the subject talking or thinking and not doing, then there is no real danger, only true emotions.

PERSONAL POWER AND BODY LANGUAGE

During the verbal confrontation stage, many people get nervous and jumpy. An aggressor will feed off this fear and inability to maintain control over the situation. If he can lead you into a state of fear, anger, weakness, confusion, or frustration, then *he* has gained control of the situation.

As a professional, you must first control your inner self by taking a deep breath and relaxing your shoulders. Slow your body movements down so that you don't look guarded or jumpy. Your demeanor should be natural, smooth, and controlled. This does not mean you should *not* use an aggressive approach, because in some cases strong, assertive communication can be effective. But if you stay cool, the subject may doubt his ability to fluster you and question whether he has chosen the right person to attack. He may wonder why you are so calm and imagine you have backup or that you are more streetwise than he is.

Many times the subject will back away, but he will do it boastfully to make others think he hasn't been frightened off. If this happens, do not press the issue, because you have already gained control and mentally restrained him. *The true art of restraining or self-defense is to control the situation without physically touching the subject.*

In a confrontation, you do not want to give the impression that you are preparing to restrain the subject or protect yourself, although your mind must be set and ready to make the move if necessary. Proper body language—including facial expressions, body position, and your tone of voice—can give you the element of surprise here. Standing with your feet wide apart and holding your hands in half-clenched fists could provoke a physical confrontation because it is a tense and aggressive stance. On the other hand, keeping your feet at a natural, narrow width with your shoulders relaxed and hands open may give off signals of passiveness—the aggressor could view you as being defenseless and a likely victim to overpower, overlooking the fact that you are, in fact, mentally prepared.

Either way, if the subject moves toward you, he will do so open and off guard. This gives you the upper hand, because he does not know when or how you will strike, and he will be vulnerable to restraining holds or self-defense techniques. Usually, however, by standing naturally and acting confidently, the aggressor will sense you know something more than he does or that you do not feel intimidated and thus leave you alone.

A final hint: in an interview, confrontation, or crisis intervention, the subject may try to direct you away from the topic by leading the conversation or displaying body language different from his motives. If he is known to always have someone with him, or you are interviewing one subject apart from the other, beware. If the situation becomes hostile, the subject may misdirect you so his accomplice can attack.

EYE CONTACT

If the subject has escalated the situation to the point where it may get physical, direct eye contact should usually be avoided. (This is not the case when you are actively trying to defuse a situation, as described later.) Some aggressors have a wild, hypnotic gaze, and looking into their eyes could cause you to sway from your plan and deflate your spirit and will to make the necessary restraining tactic. This is not always the rule, however. Looking away from the subject at a key moment could give the impression of a lack of confidence, giving him increased confidence to continue his assaultive behavior.

Rather than looking directly into his eyes, look between them or choose a spot on his face near the eyes such as the eyebrows, nose, forehead, or cheekbone. Look *through* your subject's face and not at it. This will make you appear spiritless and empty hearted, sending no vibration for your subject to read. It will also cast an "empty" emotion over you. When you experience this empty emotion you will have no fear of being attacked.

Eye contact can be used to keep the subject in temporary check. This is done by not looking directly at him at first, then suddenly looking directly into his eyes wildly. For a split second he will be hypnotized and motionless, providing you with a prime opportunity to restrain him.

RESTRAINING AND PROTECTING

To restrain generally means to control or check, or to limit or restrict. To protect means to keep from harm or injury, or to guard. But in the world of managing assaultive behavior, these words have more specific definitions. Restrain means to decrease someone's ability to harm himself or others. Protect means to decrease injury to yourself or others while preventing the total success of an attack.

For example, if a subject intends to assault you, you protect yourself by trying to decrease the number of strikes that land on vital areas of your body and minimize the extent of your injuries. If a subject is attempting to harm himself or others, instead of counterattacking you restrain him by using approved holds, locks, takedowns, or, ideally, verbal distraction until you can gain control of the situation.

GENERAL TIPS

If you have just encountered a hostile subject, have been attacked, or are forced to enter a potentially risky situation (e.g., an investigation in a high-crime area), follow these tips:

1) Don't take your normal route home, and try to stay in populated, well-lit areas.
2) Look carefully inside your vehicle before getting inside. Criminals have been known to gain access to cars, hide inside, and relock the doors, giving you the impression that all is as you left it.
3) When walking, look ahead for blind spots and other trouble areas and avoid them.
4) Take wide loops around corners.
5) Don't walk close to doorways or in poorly lit areas.
6) Walk near the curb on sidewalks that have bushes, or walk on the inside if cars are parked too close to the curb.
7) When in a parking garage or lot, look under the cars near yours to see if anyone's crouching or laying nearby.
8) If you think you are being followed, go into a well-populated business area or double back in the opposite direction to see if you are being followed. If you are, then go to the nearest police or fire department, friend's home, or business, and call the police.
9) At home, before opening your door to a visitor, especially at night, look first and ask who is there. If you are fearful, equip yourself with a weapon, plan an escape, yell out "the police are on the way," say nothing else, and call

911. Once connected to the police, do not hang up the phone even if you have to flee. The police can trace your location and continue to monitor sounds in your home with the phone line open.

10) If someone taps you on the shoulder, take a large step away at an angle before turning around. If you don't, you may turn right into a sucker punch or knife.

11) Document everything regarding an assault or whatever it was that caused you fear. Write down the who, what, when, where, why, and how. Then tell more than one person about the incident.

12) If an assault or threat has taken place, report it to the police and obtain a restraining order if they advise you to.

CHAPTER 2

THE AGGRESSOR

There are three general categories of aggressors: verbal, physical, and combination aggressors. The verbal aggressor intimidates through words, uses body language to intensify his threat, and has the potential to inflict bodily harm. The physical aggressor inflicts bodily harm without warning. The combination aggressor uses verbal threats and body language to intimidate and will hype himself up to the point where he will inflict bodily harm on another person.

Verbal and combination aggressors often launch assaults in a spontaneous and emotional manner. The physical aggressor will assault in a premeditated and unprovoked fashion. All three have the potential to be destructive to property as well as people, and all three have the potential to use weapons.

THE VERBAL AGGRESSOR

The average subject generally falls into the verbal or combination category. His behavior is influenced by emotions and feelings. His anger and assaultive behavior is generally spontaneous, not premeditated. He needs to be psyched up and provoked before attacking.

In the talking stage, the subject can be unassertive but otherwise bold, such as displaying stubbornness or intentional inefficiency. He can also be assertive and ready to debate. He may attempt to humiliate you in public or harm you emotionally by saying things that hurt your feelings, including name calling, using gender or racial slurs, insulting your intelligence, and questioning your femininity or masculinity.

The verbal aggressor constantly observes and analyzes your body language and may change his behavior to obtain a certain response from you. He may, for example, use a soft, pleasant, cooperative voice, then suddenly explode loudly. He may get harsh, loud, and profane, then suddenly switch to an apologetic tone. He may use a monotone or robotic style of speaking.

Some subjects can turn irrational and speak in "word salad," mixing a variety of topics together during the conversation. They may also speak in gibberish or extremely rapidly. (These are also signs of mental illness or street drug use.) Other subjects may be higher functioning or stabilized on medication and not display these signs.

Beware of the type of verbal aggressor who uses deceit and manipulation to gain your trust. He will sound nonthreatening and smooth and use body language that displays compassion and friendship, but at the same time he will be looking for the opportunity to strike you or influence others to cause you harm.

THE PHYSICAL AGGRESSOR

The physical aggressor can strike without warning or launch a preplanned attack on you. You must be ready for either a direct or sneak attack. You usually won't have time to use talk-down techniques. If you know the person's history, upon contact immediately get him to talk, and try to build some rapport. But beware: at times he can appear very submissive and then suddenly assault you. These people can also become stalkers.

Some physical aggressors need support from others before they attack. He may seem passive when alone, but with another person he becomes confident and aggressive. Gang members are an example: they are more dangerous when in a group. Therefore, as a general rule, avoid trying to intervene with groups and instead always attempt to interact on a one-to-one basis.

OTHER TYPES

Subjects who abuse alcohol and drugs can display unpredictable behavior. This type of aggressor becomes more volatile the more he abuses the substance, and he can respond without thinking of the consequences.

Another type of subject who is very volatile is the reserved, quiet, introverted type. When he reacts negatively, it is like an explosion, with uncontrolled, irrational rage. These people can become homicidal or self-destructive.

A final example of an aggressor is one who uses your friends and loved ones to attack you indirectly. He will find ways to disrupt your family life or damage your standing at work. He will do things like start painful rumors or manipulate people around you through lies and deception. His motive is to get others to harm you for him. He doesn't care if you are harmed physically, emotionally, or financially.

CHAPTER 3

BODY LANGUAGE

Now that you have been briefed on who the aggressor is, let's talk about his body language. These are the telltale signs of impending violence that raise the red flag. If you can spot the signs, you'll know when to begin defusing the situation.

Nonverbal communication is conveyed through body language on a conscious or subconscious level. On a conscious level, for example, people indicate "yes" with an upward/downward head movement. "I don't know" may be communicated by a shoulder shrug. These body movements are understood even without the spoken word.

Subconscious body language conveys a message about the sender, but these nonverbal signs often portray a meaning different from the subject's spoken word. For example, a subject may say that he is not nervous or under stress, but at the same time his foot and leg is bouncing up and down rapidly. Another suspect may confess to a crime and claim that no one else was involved, yet he won't make eye contact with the interviewer when pressed about accomplices. Yet another suspect may claim innocence during an interrogation while constantly rubbing his sweaty palms together or wiping them on his clothing. The sender of nonverbal messages is seldom aware that his body is giving out these signs, all of which indicate lying or deception.

In an interview or confrontational situation, you should begin reading the subject's body language immediately. Knowing how to recognize nonverbal cues will provide you with the insight to know when to defuse or, if necessary, restrain a hostile subject. Reading body language is also an excellent tool to assess an individual's character.

SIGNS OF STRESS AND DECEPTION

It is important to be able to recognize the telltale signs of agitation so that you will be in a position to defend yourself or restrain the subject if necessary. In an interview, it is difficult to know if the question you are about to ask is going to be interpreted as threatening. After being asked a series of questions, the subject may feel boxed in and start to lie or begin contemplating a physical assault.

If a subject is sitting and starts experiencing increased stress, he may shift positions often, shuffle his feet, cross and uncross his legs, fiddle with his fingers, dig his fingers into the palm of the opposite hand, touch parts of his face, or play with his hair. Folding the arms across the chest is a sign of being uncooperative or defensive. A deceptive person's rate of speech may increase and his tone of voice may rise. If a subject maintains a steady rhythm when responding to questioning and then changes this pattern with brief silence or vocal pauses like "uh" or repeats the question before answering, this usually indicates deception. Such pauses are used to buy the subject time to regain his composure and reduce stress. A subject who is trying to convince you that he is being truthful will sometimes raise his voice.

Watch a subject's mouth. Fake smiles are usually spotted easily, but if the subject is experienced at deception, it can be difficult to catch. A fake smile usually only shows the top teeth; natural smiles show both the upper and lower teeth. Grinding the teeth; biting the cheek, lip, or tongue; and fake smiles are signs of tension or stress.

If a subject is always maintaining eye contact but suddenly, after being asked a targeted question, breaks eye contact, this usually means the answer will not be true or will be deceptive. This is not always the rule, however: the question asked or the answer the subject is about to give could simply be embarrassing to him. And always remember: the person who has no regard for the rights of others, is irrational, or is a career criminal can often look you directly in the eye and lie. He can also smile and then assault you with no remorse.

SIGNS OF IMPENDING VIOLENCE

Telltale signs of a potentially assaultive subject include extreme pacing, the inability to keep his arms or hands in one position, wide stance, jutting chest, erect body posture, fixed eyes, speaking to himself, rapid speech, changes in speech volume, refusing to cooperate, looking at you out of the corner of his eye, the inability to maintain a relaxed facial expression, and leaving the area and then returning to stalk you or another intended victim. Bent legs or a bobbing motion are signs that the subject is preparing to spring at you. Long pauses in the middle of a sentence could be a sign that the subject is contemplating an attack. Pacing behind you or outside your vision (i.e., in a blind spot) are signs of a possible sneak attack. If a subject looks you over from the top of your head down to your feet, he may be sizing you up for an attack. Hitting a fist into the open palm, having a tense body, or rubbing a clenched fist with the opposite hand are intimidation gestures.

A person who shows signs of persecution, jealousy, suspiciousness, mistrust, and combativeness may see the professional (i.e., one who must deal with controntational behavior as part of his job) as a threat to his health, freedom, status in life, or finances and could lash out violently. He could think that everybody is out to get him and nobody wants to help. He may develop the illusion that you are someone who he hates or has once hurt him. Your job and professional status may represent an institution or agency that once opposed him.

Extreme friendliness, especially after the subject has received negative information or a "no" answer, profuse apologizing, waving hello more than usual, shaking hands a lot during the conversation, and a friendly slap or punch as a sign of "you're OK" are all signs that the subject is attempting to gain your trust. He is trying to get you to relax and feel comfortable with him invading your personal space before launching a premeditated assault.

Listen for borderline verbal threats and then observe the subject's body language for confirmation. Such statements could include references to weapons, violence, and fear. Phrases like, "You don't look so tough," or, "I can do anything I want," could be a challenge or threat.

Tension and stress will cause physiological changes in the subject's body. A dry mouth, redness in the face, enlarged vein or artery pulsing in the neck or temple area, eye or mouth twitch, rapid eye fluttering, heavy or erratic breathing, widening of the eyes, and exposing a lot of the white of the eyes are signs that the subject is losing control and may attack.

Look for any signs of the subject being under the influence of alcohol or drugs. For example, check out the eyes. Do they look unfocused during conversation? Are they glazed? Are the pupils tightly constricted? All are signs of alcohol or drug use.

Preattack Indicators Used By Law Enforcement

The following preattack indicators are taught to law enforcement personnel by officer Don Gulla.

Conspicuous ignoring. Suspect is aware of the officer's presence but is ignoring his verbal commands. Example: officer is commanding suspect to stop walking away but suspect ignores the officer and continues to walk.

Looking around. Suspect is looking around instead of at the officer. Suspect is looking for witnesses, weapons, friends to help, escape routes, etc.

Verbal threats of assault. Suspect is making verbal threats to assault officer or is telling the officer that he won't be arrested.

Excessive emotional attitude. Subject is showing excessive emotion during contact, may be combined with verbal threats. Not to be confused with a victim of a crime who is emotionally upset over the event.

Unreasonableness. Subject is acting in a manner which under the circumstances is unreasonable. Example: officer contacts subject during traffic stop and asks him to step out of the car. Subject refuses the reasonable request.

Alcohol and/or drug use. Subject is under the influence of alcohol and/or drugs. According to the 1997 U.S. Department of

---

Preattack Postures

Bladed stance. Subject is standing with one foot forward and one foot back. This stance is often used in sports or martial arts.

Hand set. Clenching and unclenching of hands into a fist. Subject is probably unaware he is doing it.

Shoulder shift. Upper body twist bringing one shoulder forward and one back. Example: suspect is cocking arm back to throw a punch.

Head drop. Chin comes down toward collarbone. Suspect may appear to be looking up at you.

Target glance. Suspect is looking at a target before the assault. Example: suspect staring at police officer's gun in its holster before attempting to grab it.

Thousand-yard stare. If subject is looking at you, it appears that he is looking past you into the distance.

NOTE: Cultural differences play an important part in what message body language is giving out. A positive gesture in our culture could be considered taboo in another culture or vice versa. If your subject is from a different culture, do some research into this area prior to interviewing or observing him.

A real-life example illustrates this point. A social worker once made an allegation of child abuse against some parents who were immigrants from an Asian country. There were marks or scratches on their child, so the social worker suspected inappropriate discipline. It was later discovered that in their country coins were used to scratch the skin as a healing ritual. Upon learning this, the social worker rescinded his complaint and educated the family in acceptable behavior in the United States.

Justice/FBI publication *In the Line of Fire: Violence against Law Enforcement,* 62 percent of offenders were using alcohol and/or drugs before assaulting a police officer.

Violent history. Suspect has history of being assaultive, especially against police officers.

YOUR BODY LANGUAGE

Understanding body language can help you to better convey your own message to the listener. During a confrontation, interview, or interrogation, the subject is also trying to learn about you by observing your mannerisms and judging your confidence, professionalism, and control. It is important to know how the tone of your voice, facial expressions, gestures, and posture can tell a story about who you are or what you are trying to accomplish.

Good body language for a professional is to face your subject and maintain eye contact. Let him know he has your full attention. Keep your arms unfolded and shoulders relaxed. Have an erect but not rigid posture. Stay at least one arm's length plus an extra foot away from the subject. Be relaxed but attentive. Speak in a clear, moderate tone of voice, but not in a monotone. Be well groomed and wear professional attire.

Waving your arms or hands or pointing your finger can cause a subject to feel uncomfortable. If you do this frequently, try to control it; a subject might think you are trying to take a swing at him. Again, it's a good idea to stand at least an arm's length plus an extra foot away, which will help the subject interpret your body movements, give you reaction time in case he decides to advance toward you, and increase your ability to observe him for telltale signs of stress or impending violence. Also, keeping a proper distance ensures that you won't misinterpret any of *his* arm waving as an attack. It would not be right if you restrained or used a self-defense move, only to find out that the subject talks a lot with his hands.

• • • • •

Once you become unguarded, especially when communicating with an irrational person or a person with a violent history, you become a potential victim. Practice your ability to spot nonverbal cues by studying other people's body language whenever possible. Being able to recognize, interpret, and evaluate nonverbal communication can provide you with a distinct advantage in defusing a hostile situation.

CHAPTER 4

ASPECTS OF
ASSAULTIVE BEHAVIOR

A subject who becomes assaultive usually will have a reason for doing so. Whether his reason is justified or not, as a professional you need to understand what triggers him to become assaultive and how to best respond to each phase of his escalating violent behavior.

Being physically harmed or the threat of being harmed are the most common reasons for a subject to become combative. Visual or auditory hallucinations are also typical reasons. Sometimes a subject may become angered by who you represent—he could have been wronged, whether it be real or imagined, by an institution, government agency, corporation, law enforcement department, or court system, and, since you are employed by the offending entity, he may take out his hostility on you. Name calling, restricted privileges, general frustration, flashbacks, alcohol or drug abuse, and reaction to medication are other examples of things that trigger assaultive behavior.

PHASES OF ASSAULTIVE BEHAVIOR

Once a subject is triggered, he will start displaying the telltale body language signs. This is where you'll observe pacing, tense or unnatural facial expressions, verbal abuse (including racial/ethnic slurs, gender slurs, profanity, and threats), changes in voice, stalking, talking to self, being disruptive, and so forth. This is a good phase for early intervention, where you should get the person talking before he starts doing and defuse the situation before it escalates to physical violence.

If early intervention is not performed or is not successful, the subject may become even more verbally and physically assaultive. He may harm himself, destroy property, or target a specific person at random to attack. This is the phase where a talk down or a show of force is necessary (discussed further in Chapter 5). If the situation explodes to physical violence, deploy your professional assault response team if applicable, or group as many personnel together as possible and discuss restraining strategies. Once you have formed a plan, take immediate action.

After you have defused or managed the assaultive behavior and the subject is under physical/mental control, you must maintain an on-guard but empathetic composure. The subject may be fatigued, remorseful, embarrassed, and/or depressed, or he may re-escalate. He may cry out, seclude himself, regress, go to sleep, or become suicidal.

ASSAULTIVE BEHAVIOR BY AGE GROUP

In my opinion, assaultive behavior is increasing among young people. Gang activity and drugs are two major reasons for this. I also believe that some of the television shows, movies, and music of the younger generation has a greater level of violent and sexual suggestions, and the world would be a better place if emphasis in movies and music could be placed more on good moral character, friendship, awareness that there are consequences for behavior, respect for authority, and love for mankind. Unfortunately, sex and violence sell tickets and generate good ratings.

In order for us to understand the spectrum of assaultive behavior, we must look at it in terms of age groups. The following are general guidelines that I've learned from my professional assault response training:

- Preschool-age children have difficulty controlling outbursts of anger. They are easily provoked and act out after being told "no." Environmental conditions such as cold, heat, hunger, and family dysfunction contribute to this behavior.

- Elementary school-age children have more control. They are intelligent enough to fight when adult intervention is not readily available. Peer pressure begins to play an important role. Violence is seldom malicious, and hitting usually is confined to the body rather than the head.

- Adolescents tend to defy authority. They may have difficulty making the right choices. Fighting can become more malicious. Older adolescents begin to channel aggressive behavior more competitively. This age is at risk to gang, alcohol, and drug involvement. Boy/girl relationships could spark violence. Peer pressure is stronger.

- Young adults experience less impulsive acts of violence outside of their circle of family and friends, although minor disagreements can still provoke violence. Drug and alcohol abuse contributes to lack of self-control.

- Middle-aged adults rarely have the impulse to fight, although domestic issues, threat to property or livelihood, alcoholism, and other factors can trigger assaultive behavior.

- Elderly adults usually avoid physical confrontations, but physical and mental issues can contribute to impulsive aggressive behavior and sometimes deep emotional responses.

BASIC COMMUNICATION MODEL OF
ASSAULTIVE BEHAVIOR

Basically, there are two extremes of communication that identify a subject as being a high risk of assaultive behavior. At one end of the model is a subject who displays a passive approach. This type of person may have a quiet demeanor, desire to be alone, and poor self-care. He may stare, blame others, sabotage plans, whine, complain, talk to himself, or harm himself. On the other end of the model is a subject who is more openly hostile, uses verbal threats, displays an angry demeanor, and is destructive to property.

As a professional, the question you must ask is how do you communicate with subjects displaying these two different types of behavior. The answer falls in the middle of the model. This means you must display confidence, but not in an arrogant manner. Be assertive but nonthreatening. To accomplish this, always be organized and in control. Before you make contact with the subject, plan each stage of your intervention. Display the authority, knowledge, and confidence of a professional. With a professional attitude and the ability to defuse and restrain assaultive behavior, your colleagues will admire you, clients and subjects will respect you, and the combative person will be managed successfully.

ENVIRONMENTAL CONDITIONS

People react to various conditions of their environment. It can be too hot or cold, too dark or light, or too quiet or noisy. You can be waiting too long for service, the room could be overcrowded, or it could have an unbearable odor. Some people want boundaries, guidance, and structure, but instead their environment is disorganized. Others want independence and freedom to do as they please, but instead their environment is too structured. These are examples of environmental conditions contributing to tension, frustration, hostility, and ultimately assaultive behavior.

In a professional environment such as a mental health facility or correctional institution, staffing problems could create a hostile situation. Examples include staff being inconsistent with enforcing rules and procedures, staff undermining each other, not enough staff on duty, lack of proper documentation, staff's inability to supervise themselves, or lack of activities for the subjects to participate in.

If you are confronted with a hostile subject, analyze the environment for factors that may be contributing to his behavior. You may be able to use the results of this evaluation to negotiate a compromise and prevent or decrease hostility and physical injury to the subject and yourself.

MODEL OF BASIC NEEDS AND REASONS

An aggressive subject has basic needs that have to be filled in order for him to maintain balance. If this balance is not maintained, he could initiate violence. If the professional threatens any of his basic needs, the chance of assaultive behavior from the subject is increased.

One basic consideration is the need to be safe; if the subject feels his safety is jeopardized, than he may do anything to protect himself. A subject could also become violent if he is making a last-ditch effort to obtain a given need. A sense of belonging, love, and self-esteem are other elements of the basic needs model.

In order to understand why a person may assault, whether his reasons are justified or not, put yourself into his shoes. The subject could be experiencing fear of attack or of loss. He could have reached a stage of frustration and exploded rather then sought help. His desire for something could be so overpowering that he attempts to manipulate his surroundings; if manipulation fails, he may become violent. Other subjects only know intimidation tactics as a way to get their needs fulfilled, and when intimidation fails, they become violent.

When a person is triggered into assaultive behavior, he feels he is at a point of no return and his survival skills go into action. As a professional, you need to present a way out in a nonthreatening, nondemeaning manner. Direct him in a way that makes him feel you are concerned for his safety and, with help, he can work his way past this crisis. Reassure the subject that things will only get better with his cooperation and ability to regain self-control.

When it comes to analysis of and response to assaultive behavior, every situation has its own variables and dynamics. Learning from personal experiences in the field, being tutored by a seasoned professional, and practicing case scenarios are the only ways you will be able to improve your defusing and tactical skills.

RESPONSE PROCEDURE

When the situation requires immediate intervention, an appropriate response procedure needs to be implemented. The main questions are, when do you use hands-on tactics, and how much force is "reasonable force"? (These topics will be discussed in more detail in upcoming chapters.)

Basically, if a hostile subject is only being verbal, then use verbal intervention. If the subject is displaying assaultive behavior but is not causing physical harm to himself or others, then use show of force or evasive tactics, and place the professional assault team on standby if applicable to your situation. If the subject is harmful to himself or others, then use hands-on restraining tactics, or activate the professional assault team.

Once again, verbal hostility includes name calling, using profanity, making threats, debating, passive resistance, and refusal to follow directives. Assaultive behavior includes verbal threats with the means and ability to carry through with the threat (e.g., a subject threatening to kill you who has the strength and/or a weapon to do so), property damage, a less-than-malicious attack (e.g., striking or kicking with no contact to a person or himself), and invading the safety zone of others. Causing harm to himself or others includes the subject having physical contact with others with intent to harm, pushing others into objects or to the floor, any type of striking with contact, use of weapons, throwing bodily fluids like blood or urine, spitting, and kicking or punching with no contact but with intent to injure.

CHAPTER 5

DEFUSING A
HOSTILE SITUATION

In order to defuse a hostile situation, you need to get the subject's attention and keep it. Once you have obtained his attention, you have control over the situation. At this point, you need to decrease his agitation and tactfully lead him into gaining self-control.

GETTING THE SUBJECT'S ATTENTION

Getting the subject's attention is a science and, in most cases, is done through an indirect approach, i.e., without letting him know your true intentions. In some situations a direct approach such as asking him to calm down will work, but in a hostile confrontation this could enrage the subject. Most aggressors do not believe or realize that they are escalating a situation or are out of control. So a more indirect approach is necessary.

Some professionals call this indirect approach the "back door" because the subject doesn't see you coming in that way. All of a sudden you have his attention and he is discussing exactly what he didn't want to discuss in the first place.

FINDING HIS MOTIVATION

One method of gaining the subject's attention is to find out what motivates him. This technique is used by private investigators when attempting to obtain information from willing or unwilling subjects.

Please note that the following are generalizations based on my past experiences. My intention is not to stereotype people but to give the reader a basic understanding of one method of profiling individuals (i.e., learning to think like them) to help better understand their behavior. Obviously, not all people in these categories will always display these motivations.

Pencil pushers. People who do a lot of paperwork are motivated by fewer problems and less work.

Businesspeople. Motivated by getting more business and increased sales.

Public image people. Motivated by anything that will associate their name with something positive or special or that will get their name mentioned in the media.

Criminals. Motivated by money and power.

Outgoing people. Motivated by friends, fun, status, money, and job security.

Caregivers, helpers, teachers. Motivated by a desire to help people.

Religious people. Motivated by love, spiritual development, guilt, and conviction.

The mentally ill. Motivated by attention, money, cigarettes, or any person, place, thing, or thought that they hold valuable over all other things.

BUILDING RAPPORT

Another method of holding a subject's attention is to develop rapport. The keys to building rapport are patience, getting the subject to think you have something in common with him, and establishing a bond between the two of you.

To build rapport, try to find something that interests the subject that you can discuss with him. It could be anything—life experiences, school, food, stores, movies, children, cars, cities/states, music, hobbies, sports, or jobs. Compliment the way the subject is dressed or his intelligence, hair, or jewelry. Get him to talk about himself or something he likes. If you find out he likes to cook, play sports, or write poetry or music, get him to educate you. Most people think they are in control if they are placed into the teacher role.

Another technique to build rapport is to mirror the speech and mannerisms of the subject. This is commonly used in undercover work. Because you are a professional, the subject already knows who you are, so in this case to mirror means to speak the language of the subject. If he is one whose thoughts and interests are directed inward (i.e., an introvert), take it slow. If he is interested in others or in the environment (i.e., an extrovert), be talkative. If he understands things in simple terms, don't be technical; speak in plain language. If his body language is relaxed, you relax. You are trying to make him think that you are like him.

When talking to a subject, don't be threatening, and don't let the situation reach the stage of aggression. If he does become agitated but you had already established some type of rapport before that point, it will be easier to regain control. If the subject has made any kind of connection with you, this will be the door for you to reconnect with him during the hostile stage.

PRELIMINARY STRATEGY

Recognizing the telltale signs and knowing the right words to say and the right body language to project are not the only aspects of defusing. The professional must know how to face the hostile subject and how to exit if the intervention fails.

In my violence prevention workshops I teach three preliminary steps to proper defusing: one, maintain a safe distance; two, look for weapons nearby; three, look for exits.

Maintain a safe distance. A safe distance is at least one arm's length plus. With your palms open and arms stretched forward, try to calm the person down. Take a step away for safety. (Stepping away also shows a passive, nonaggressive attitude.) Then try turning your palms up in a pleading fashion or putting them together in a prayerful manner and say something like, "I'm sorry. I don't want to fight. I apologize if I have offended you." Adapting this manner and phrasing should help decrease hostility.

Look for weapons. Look for both obvious and improvised weapons that could be used against you, to include any items the subject could use to hit, cut, stab, shoot, or club you with. You must prevent him from getting to these weapons. Likewise, take note of tables or chairs that you can stand behind or use as a shield. Any such obstacles that will slow the attacker down are important.

If you can't prevent the subject from getting a weapon, by noting where the weapons are you will at least be able to arm yourself as well. An attacker considers a weapon as a mental and physical advantage, especially when you are unarmed. Once he sees that you are also armed, it takes away this advantage. (NOTE: Professionals must use caution here for liability reasons. Nonetheless, anyone, professional or civilian, who is wedged into a life-threatening situation must be aware of all of his self-defense options.)

Look for exits. If you decide to run instead of fight, you must already have a plan of escape in mind. Even if the situation causes you to deliver an aggressive self-defense technique, you will have already planned an exit.

INTERVIEW DEFUSING TECHNIQUES

When interviewing a subject face to face as a private investigator or in any official capacity, try to do it at his home or somewhere where he will feel comfortable. Avoid an office setting— an attorney's or PI's office, police department, courtroom conference area, or the subject's place of employment may cause him stress, and he may lose his willingness to speak openly. You want the atmosphere to be relaxed so the subject feels in control and not threatened.

If you are dealing with a subject who you believe will become agitated or hostile, try not to crowd his personal space. Stand or sit in a manner that's not confrontational. Place yourself at a comfortable distance and at a slight angle to him. If another investigator is with you, have him sit or stand in an open manner that shares information, such as a triangle or circle seating arrangement. Other times the second investigator can sit farther away, take notes, and follow your lead if necessary.

If the subject gets hostile, try to reassure him that you are not there to persecute or make judgment; all you are trying to do is find the truth, and you are hoping he can help. Then back off from an aggressive style of questioning and attempt to speak about something more comfortable, less personal, and less threatening. Listen to his concerns and show true empathy for his feelings. If this defuses the situation, reestablish rapport and begin asking nonthreatening questions. If all this fails, reschedule the interview or prepare to restrain him if things get physical and you are unable to retreat.

INTERVENTION DEFUSING TECHNIQUES

As a registered counselor and former mental health technician working with mentally ill offenders, I handled face-to-face interventions similar to my PI strategy. I tried not to crowd the irrational person. I showed open palms and used arm gestures that represented openness, concern, and caring. I sat or stood in a manner that invited conversation rather than confrontation. I left a path where the subject could walk away without incident.

When doing crisis intervention where the irrational person is very agitated, has the potential to assault someone, or has already assaulted someone, different approaches are taken. One method is to have the person who has the most history with the subject intervene and make first contact. This is done because the subject needs to communicate with someone he knows, has rapport with, and trusts. This person tries to talk the subject down by letting him vent his anger, realize his wrongdoing, voluntarily gain control of himself, and accept responsibility for his actions.

This intervention is done from a safe distance of at least 10 feet. Any other members of the team should stand nearby in case the lead person needs hands-on assistance. If the talk down is successful and physical restraint tactics are not needed, the subject is then medicated and placed into a quiet area to decrease external stimuli. If this is unsuccessful and the situation escalates, a show of force is implemented.

SHOW OF FORCE

Before physical holds or restraints are used, one more step needs to be attempted to give the subject a chance to correct his own behavior. This step is called a show of force. This technique is used not only in mental health facilities but in correctional institutions and group homes for juvenile offenders.

In a show of force, a large number of workers confronts the subject with hopes that he will calm down, be more cooperative, and become receptive to a talk down. It is best if the group consists of four or more.

The intention is to show strength in numbers. The subject, in theory, is faced with a choice: either he can take the chance of physically fighting a no-win situation or comply with the directives of the team leader.

A show of force displays to the subject that force can and will be used if he is not going to cooperate. The team has the capability to physically restrain a hostile subject, but its specific mission at this point is only to imply the threat of force and not to use it.

THE "WE" ATTITUDE

Many subjects will challenge you if you confront them while alone. If confrontation is made by show of force, there's a better chance they will back off.

Therefore, you can give a verbal show of force by using words that symbolize the "we" attitude. You do this by conveying to the subject that an authoritative force stands behind you. This gives the impression that a power greater than you is speaking through you.

For example, don't say, "I don't want you to assault anyone." Instead, use words that represent power and authority. Replace "I" with words like us, department, agency, team, government, statute, law, company, director, policy, state, and city.

Other examples:

- "Agency guidelines requires us to encourage you to calm down."
- "It is against the law for you to assault anyone."
- "It is company policy for us to assist you in calming down."
- "It is the treatment team's decision that we redirect you when you display assaultive behavior."
- "Law enforcement has asked us to follow through with pressing charges."

Aside from showing the power and authority that stands behind you, you are also diverting fault away from yourself. If the subject becomes more agitated and attempts to label you as the aggressor, again fall back on the "we" attitude. Blame can now be directed at the authoritative power instead of at you.

This can also be used as a tool for reestablishing rapport. By saying, "I understand your feelings. I am only following departmental guidelines and I know how the department can be sometimes," you connect with the subject's feelings, maintain your authority, and divert his anger away from you and toward the authoritative body. If the subject's anger intensifies toward the system, you can defuse it by showing empathy for how the system can be. Then suggest that, with his cooperation, you can look into his concerns.

OUTSIDE RESOURCES

Sometimes outside resources need to be used in order to gain control and defuse a situation. Such resources include family, friends, religious groups, social organizations, and so forth. Although a particular person from one of these groups can be called to come in and literally help talk down a subject, for our purposes we rely on motivating the subject through name dropping.

Some subjects have strong convictions that are affected by peer pressure. Mentioning family or friends and how they would feel knowing how the subject is behaving could influence him into modifying his own behavior. If, for example, you know that the subject has strong religious beliefs, getting him talking about religion could be the turning point. Another person could belong to a fraternal or social group—try using the subject's status within that group as a way to talk him down.

NEGOTIATION AND OTHER STRATEGIES

If a talk down is unproductive, you may have to negotiate. To negotiate does *not* mean to lose control of the talk down, nor does it mean rewarding the subject for hostile behavior. Negotiation is about getting what *you* want. In this case, it means reestablishing control, getting the subject talking and not doing, helping him to gain self-control, and defusing the situation without resorting to physical force.

There are limits to negotiation. If the subject requests things that are unethical, immoral, illegal, against policy, or outrageously unacceptable, then you must tactfully move the conversation to something more realistic.

The approach here is to give the subject the impression that he has control of the intervention. For example, he may request that you be quiet. In the face of this, talk less, but keep him focused on the thought of self-control. He may ask you to back off. Back off, but keep him focused on decreasing agitation. Remember, your job is to defuse hostile and assaultive behavior, not encourage it.

There may be times when you have to act afraid because the subject's goal is to instill fear into people. Once the subject feels that he has caused fear in you, his aggression may decrease. There are other times, of course, when you may be extremely fearful but will need to stand with confidence and bravery. The subject may sense your strength and doubt whether he is able to scare and manipulate you.

Saying "no" to a hostile subject during negotiations is not advisable. Instead of saying no, you may need to agree with him. As an example, the subject may say he wants to beat you up. Saying, "No, I don't think so," may only provoke him into striking out or increasing his agitation. The alternative is to agree with him by saying something like, "I know you feel that way. If I were angry, I might feel the same way too." This may decrease his stress.

There will be times when all attempts to defuse a situation fail and the subject gets combative. When this happens you must choose between fight or flight. If you are being attacked, evading and escaping should be the first choice, but there are times when restraining and using violence prevention techniques must be implemented.

CHAPTER 6

RESTRAINING AND MANAGING PHYSICAL ASSAULTS

Professional assault response teams were created in order to be able to manage agitated, hostile, or combative subjects in mental health facilities. Similar assault management teams have been formed in prisons, juvenile detention centers, and other facilities that need to manage assaultive behavior. At Western State Mental Health Hospital, where I worked, the team is called "Dr. Armstrong." This special team developed hospital-approved holds, takedowns, and methods of applying restraint devices and is constantly perfecting its assault response techniques.

The team's objective is to gain control of a subject by using hands-on restraining tactics, applying physical restraint devices if necessary, and secluding the subject to reduce external stimuli. A successful team is able to accomplish this without violating the rights of the subject, avoiding injury to the subject and team members, and keeping in mind the hospital's liability concerns.

As a professional who must deal with aggressors in your line of work, your concerns should be similar: reduce the risk of liability, restrain without injury to yourself or the subject, and don't violate the subject's rights. It is my opinion that if an aggressor commits an assault against you, however, you should file charges, obtain a restraining order, and ask law enforcement to arrest the violator.

WHEN TO RESTRAIN

I cannot teach you exactly when to restrain a subject; only experience can teach you that. All I can say is that if the telltale signs of impending violence are present and your gut feeling says "do something," either make your move or leave the area.

If you decide to restrain the subject, fix your eyes on his chest or solar plexus. In this way you can see his hands and feet. His head won't jump off and hit you, so don't look there. Don't look directly at his hands or feet either, because he can fake with one and use the other. Instead, look for sudden movement toward your target areas. By using this principle, it won't matter what the subject uses to hit you—you will always be ready to protect the part of your body that is being attacked.

There are times when you *should* look at the aggressor's hands. Sometimes he will have weapons hidden in his pocket and other places. If he has his hands in his pockets and then starts to attack, don't allow his hands to come out. If the hands are out, don't let them get inside a pocket.

This does not mean that you should automatically begin a self-defense counterattack when a subject puts his hands in his pockets. Carefully weigh the circumstances before making a move. Feel the intensity of the situation and look for other telltale signs of aggression. Consider the subject's history of violence and make a rational assessment of his behavior before judging it. For example, the subject could have been taught to place his hands in his pockets as a method to control striking out, or it could be a nervous response out of frustration with the situation, or it could just be a habit. So don't be hasty and overreact; if you make the wrong decision, you could face civil or criminal charges.

My suggestion is that if the subject makes a move for his pockets quickly or in an aggressive manner and he has a history of causing harm to others, you should use the necessary restraining tactic immediately. Otherwise, simply make note of the situation verbally, such as saying, "I feel uneasy that you have placed your hands inside your pockets. You have a history of using weapons, and I think you have one now." Likewise, if his hands are hidden behind his back or his arms are folded with his hands tucked under his armpits, make a verbal note of it—he could be hiding a weapon. If the subject becomes agitated, tenses up his body, or clenches his fist, say, "Could you please calm down. You are giving me the feeling that you are going to get violent." You can also apologize if you have made him upset or angry and state that there is no reason to get physical.

If the subject was considering an attack, he will have lost his element of surprise. He would then have to replan the assault, giving you time to terminate the conversation and leave. Don't overemphasize or persist in your speculation, however, because the subject may become offended or enraged if he doesn't have a weapon or had no intention of attacking.

There will be times when you must back away from a confrontation. Maybe your gut feeling is telling you something is not right, or you are outnumbered, overpowered, or have been set up for an attack. In these cases, backing away should be your primary goal. Run if you have to. Onlookers and even you may consider this cowardly, but deep inside you'll know it would have been a mistake, if not suicide, to press the situation.

Restrain a subject only when you are ready and all the elements are in your favor. If not, back or run away. This is not cowardice; it is being safe and in control.

THE PROFESSIONAL RESTRAINING TEAM

An effective restraining team consists of four or more team members: one to grab each arm, one to restrain both legs, and one to control the body. Additional team members assist in controlling

Figure 1

the subject, handling crowd control, and applying physical
restraint devices (Figure 1).

A solo restraining process mainly consists of recognizing the
telltale signs of impending violence, disengaging from conversation, evading or absorbing the attack, running to safety, and, if necessary, applying physical holds, takedowns, or self-protection tactics.

RESTRAINING HOLDS

Restraining holds are physical methods used to gain control of
a combative subject. They are designed to prevent or decrease
harm to yourself and others.

When applying holds, do not apply pressure against the joint,
as in martial arts arm locks. Extreme pressure could cause damage
to the joint. Instead, hold the subject's arm as illustrated in Figure
2. Keep his palm turned up or away. The team member's outer
hand should be over the top of and grasping the wrist. The inside

Figure 2

Figure 3

hand comes underneath the subject's arm and supports the hold.
You maintain leverage by straightening the subject's arm and
pressing it firmly against your upper body. This hold is designed to
check the subject's strength and his ability to use it against you.
The hold should be administered by two team members, one on
each arm, as shown in Figure 3.

Figure 4

Figures 4 and 5 show different views of a one-man restraining technique utilizing a wall. This method, although effective, is questionable because of the amount of force required to

Figure 5

bend the arm back. It can and has been used, however, in cases where a solo staff member was stalked and attacked when alone.

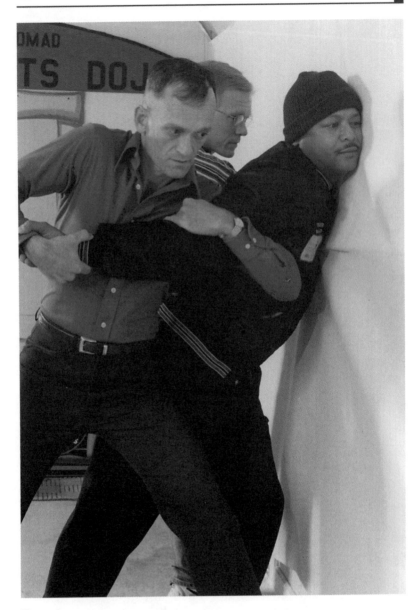

Figure 6

Figure 7

A two-man wall technique (Figures 6 and 7) is an effective way to maintain control until other team members can assist. In this position, the combative subject has no leverage to push away from the wall. Team members can lock their feet around the subject's ankles and apply leg and body weight to increase control. When applying body weight, avoid disrupting the subject's ability to breathe.

Figure 8

Figure 8 shows the incorrect way to apply an arm hold. Although common in martial arts, this technique causes too much pressure and leverage against the joint.

If the subject is being restrained while lying face-down, his arms should be turned so the palms are facing upward, as shown in Figure 9. This decreases his ability to push himself up from the floor. You can also use the two-man-against-the-wall technique, except you use the floor instead of the wall to pin him. When using the floor or wall, a third team member can assist by controlling the subject's legs or body, as shown in Figure 10.

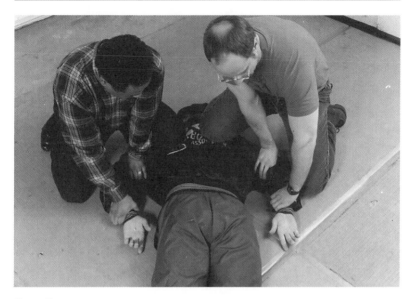

Figure 9

Figure 10

When being restrained, the subject will do anything to force you to let go. Watch out for scratching, spitting, head butting, biting, and kicking. The rule of thumb is, once you have a firm hold, do not let go. Letting go could jeopardize you or your partner's safety as well as the subject's. If you begin losing your hold, inform your partner so that he can be on guard against an attack from the subject's free hand. If this happens, it is best that both of you let go unless you are skilled at dealing with such a situation. But again, avoid letting go. It would not be good if you were restraining a subject from harming himself, then lose your hold and have him mutilate himself or someone else.

Figure 11

Instead of letting go, you can attempt to get the subject against the wall or in a corner, as shown in Figure 11. This will decrease his mobility and give you time to reposition the hold.

Self-harm or harm to others are not the only reasons why you should hold on once you have a firm grip on a subject. I remember a situation where a mentally ill patient had human feces in his hands. If my partner or I would have let go, the patient would have wiped feces all over us.

Before physical contact is made, the lead team member may need to draw the attack onto himself or get the aggressor's attention focused away from the other team members (Figure 12). Once this is done, the team is signaled by a prearranged nonverbal cue and each member grabs a preassigned limb, as shown in Figure 13. Again, any additional team members are utilized for crowd control and to apply restraint devices.

Figure 12

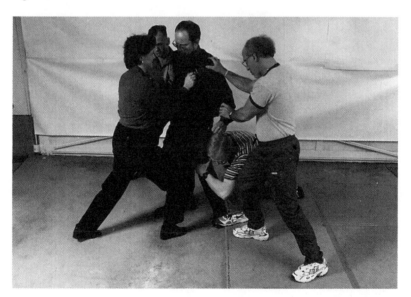

Figure 13

Figure 14

Figure 15

Figure 16

Figure 17

Sometimes while one team member draws the attack, another will intercept the subject from the rear or side and apply a bear hug technique, as shown in Figure 14. (Figure 15 shows a variation, the cross-arm bear hug.) When using the bear hug, watch out for the head butt (Figure 16). To protect against it, place your head close against the subject's body and below butting reach. Also be ready to protect yourself against a groin grab and foot or leg attacks.

If you use a traditional bear hug from the rear, there is no defense against an attack to the area below the abdomen and above the pelvic bone (Figure 17). A trained combatant will even thrust his head backward to get your guard away from the pelvis, leaving it exposed to a strike for a split second. Using the cross-arm bear hug or the team approach are safeguards against the pelvic attack.

Once you have the assaultive subject under control, you ide-ally want to get him to the floor so you can apply physical restraint devices. (Figure 18 shows a subject in four-point ambu-

latory restraints devices.)
Figure 19 shows the proper
takedown method used to
get the combative subject to
the floor. The person
assigned to the legs wraps his
arms firmly around the subject's shins to prevent him
from becoming mobile. The
arm holders prevent him
from striking or grabbing.
Considering the intensity of
the aggression, they then
maneuver the subject to the
floor in an approved manner
(i.e., considered to be of
minimal force).

Figure 18

Figure 19

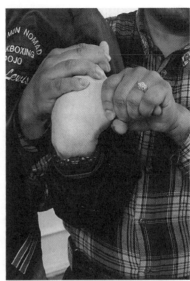

Figure 20   Figure 21

LAW ENFORCEMENT RESTRAINT TECHNIQUES

As law-abiding citizens, we should applaud the work of police officers to control crime and violent behavior. They are overworked and underpaid, but you can always count on them to protect and serve to the best of their ability.

Experienced law enforcement officers are masters at seeing the telltale signs of aggression and responding appropriately. They defuse hostile situations whenever possible, even going as far as utilizing specially trained negotiators. Sometimes the worst scenario happens and they must intervene physically, but good officers always try to use minimum force. Figures 20 and 21, for example, show two control techniques that this author has taught to law enforcement personnel that do not require a great deal of force. With both, leverage is applied to the subject's fingers and wrist to get him to comply.

The following three photo series show physical restraining tactics used by law enforcement and taught by officer Don Gulla at the Criminal Justice Training Center in Seattle, Washington. The first scenario involves a suspect attempting to grab an officer's weapon; the next two depict suspects resisting being cuffed.

Gun Retention

Figure 22. The officer is interviewing the suspect when suddenly the suspect lunges and grabs the officer's gun.

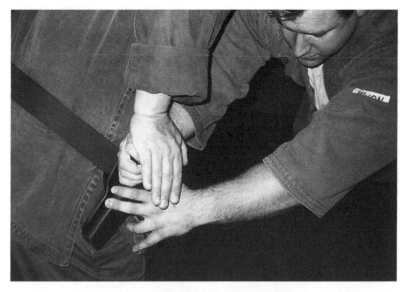

Figure 23. The officer keeps his gun in his holster by pushing the suspect's hand downward into the holster. Simultaneously, the officer steps to the left of the suspect, grabbing his elbow with his left hand and leaning beside him.

Figure 24. From this position, the officer continues to push down on the suspect's right hand as he bends the suspect's right thumb back toward him. Note that the officer's right thumb is placed on the inside of the suspect's wrist before bending the thumb.

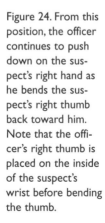
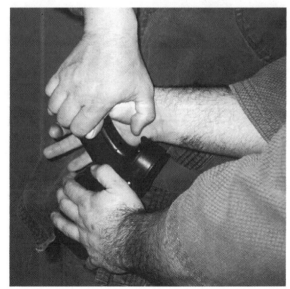

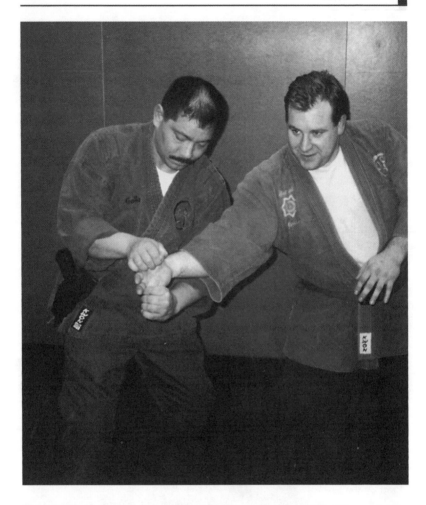

Figure 25. As the suspect releases his grip on the gun, the officer, while continuing to hold the bent thumb, quickly grabs two fingers as they slip off the gun's grip. He continues to bend the thumb as the fingers are bent in the opposite direction. This hold by itself can control some suspects.

Figure 26. Because some suspects will continue to try and disarm the officer, the officer may be required to disable the suspect. Here the officer steps with his left foot in front of the suspect as he straightens the suspect's arm over his shoulder, palm up. To disable the arm, the officer adds pressure to the thumb and fingers as he pulls the suspect's hand down toward the ground, dislocating the elbow.

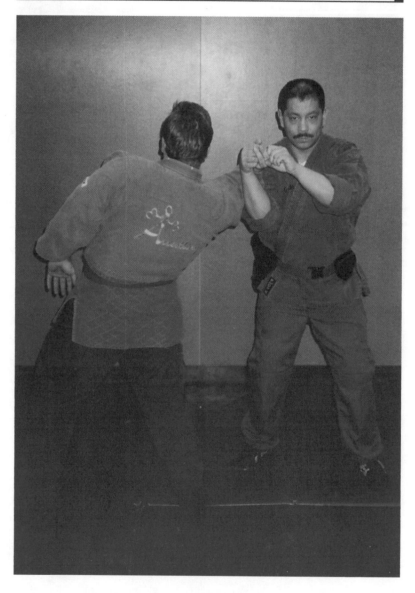

Figure 27. The officer then spins to the right as he bends the suspect's arm back.

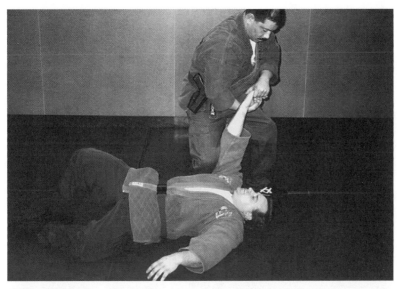

Figure 28. The officer throws the suspect backwards and straightens the suspect's arm as he lands.

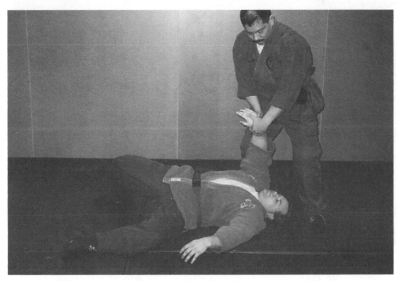

Figure 29. The officer walks around the suspect's head as he rolls him over using his right knee on the back of the suspect's upper arm.

Figure 30. The officer controls the suspect's wrist using a double wrist grab.

Figure 31. The officer kneels down to cuffing position and bends the suspect's fingers back before cuffing.

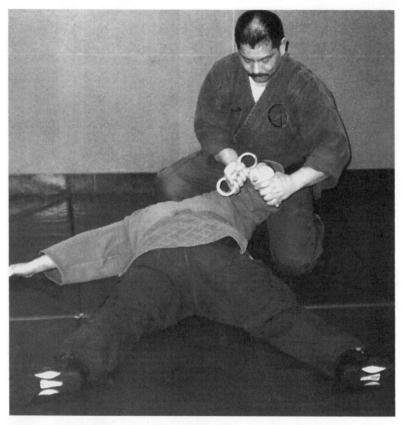

Figure 32. The officer cuffs the suspect's wrists behind his back. When the officer cuffs, he grabs only the fingers so the wrist area is exposed for cuffing.

Seated Chair Extraction

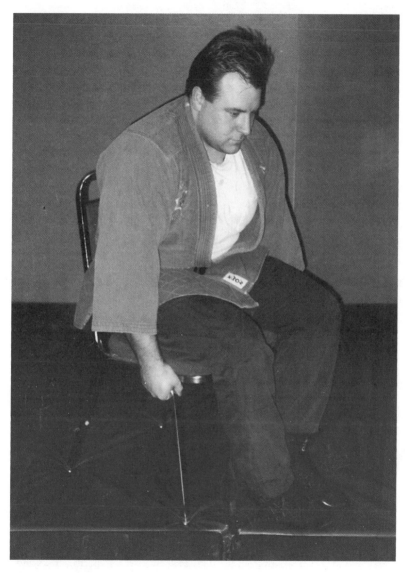

Figure 33. Suspect is seated and grabbing onto chair with both hands and won't let officers remove him from the chair to be arrested.

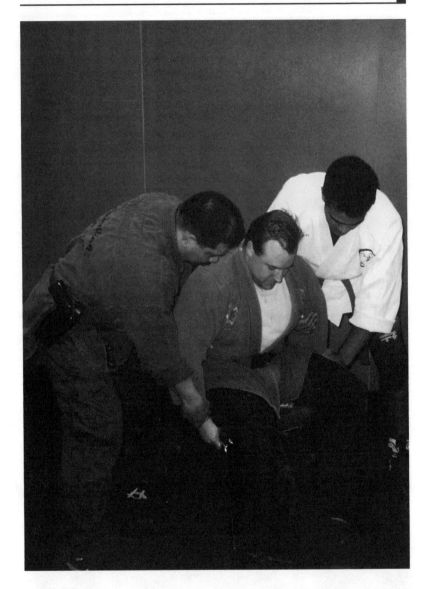

Figure 34. Officers approach from the sides and control the suspect's elbows and wrists.

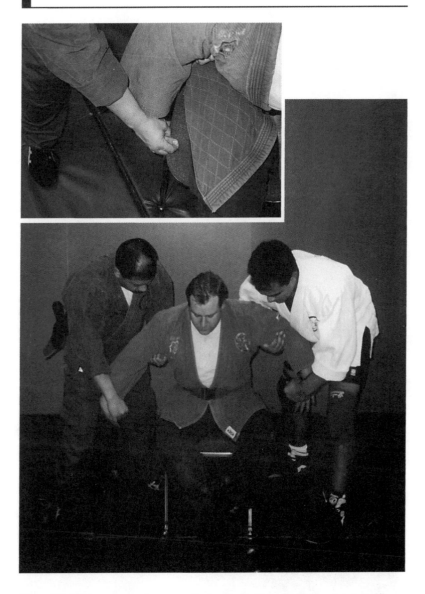

Figure 35. Officers sweep the suspect's thumbs back toward his wrists to make him release his grip on the chair.

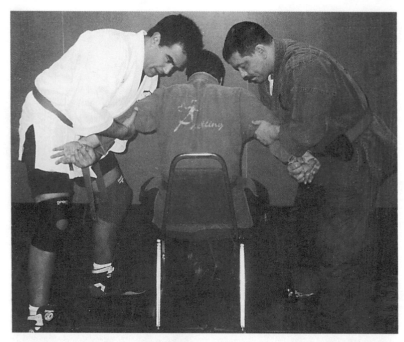

Figure 36. Keeping the suspect seated, the officers continue to hold the suspect's thumbs as they bring his hands behind the chair.

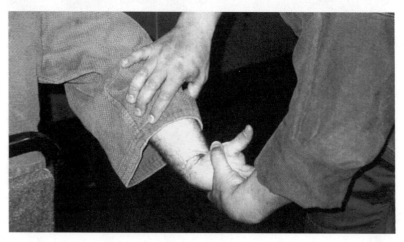

Figure 37. Officer applies a palm-forward wrist lock prior to cuffing suspect's wrist.

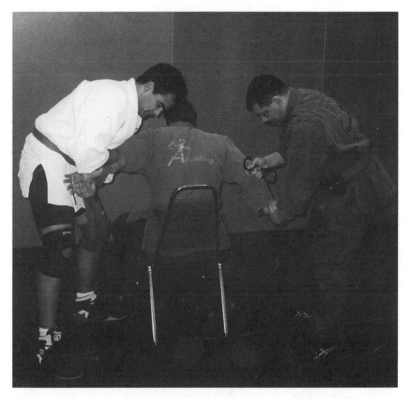

Figure 38. Officer #1 cuffs one wrist while officer #2 controls the other.

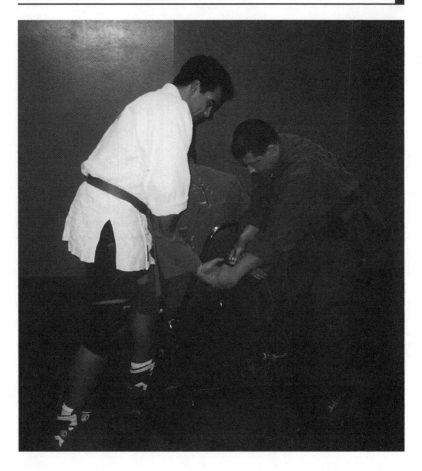

Figure 39. Officer #1 grabs suspect's fingers on second hand and cuffs second wrist.

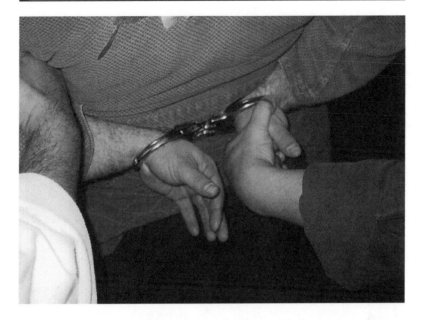

Figure 40. Officer #1 uses a gooseneck grip to escort the suspect while officer #2 controls the elbow and wrist of the other arm.

Two Officer Kneeling Arm Extraction

Figure 41. Suspect is prone on ground with hands underneath him and won't allow officer to bring his hands out to be cuffed.

Figure 42. Officer #1 (in white) uses knee to pin the suspect's arm to the ground while putting body weight on the suspect's back with his hands.

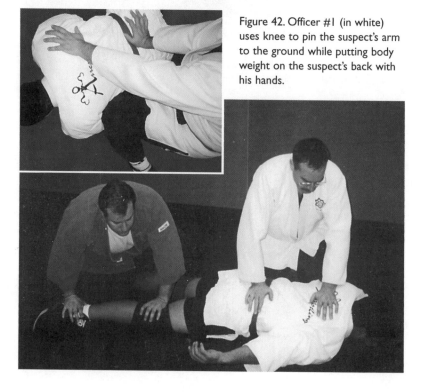

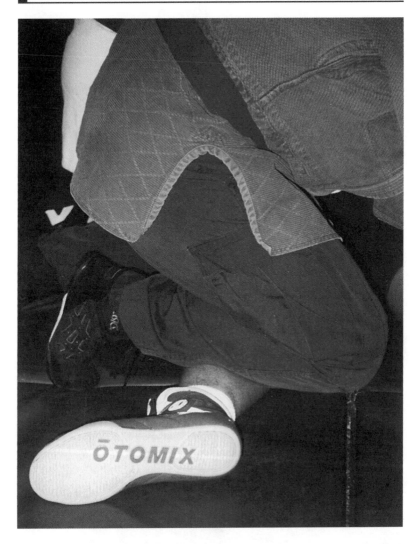

Figure 43. Officer #2 controls suspect's legs by pinning outside leg with hands and uses his shinbone to put pressure on the back of the suspect's lower calf of the other leg while being ready for a reaction from the suspect. Officer #1 orders suspect to bring his arm out from underneath.

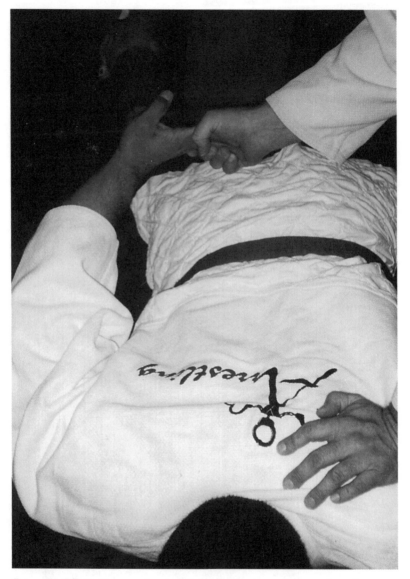

Figure 44. Officer #1 controls suspect's hand when it comes out using a finger control hold.

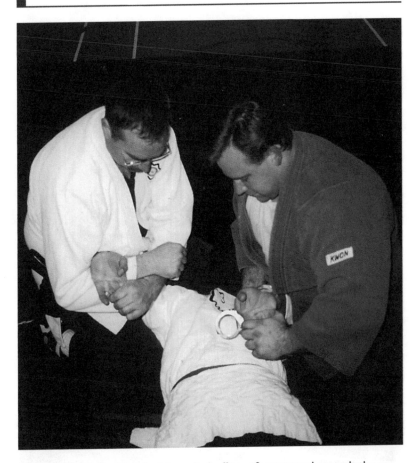

Figure 45. Once the finger lock is applied, officer #2 moves and controls the suspect's other arm and cuffs it.

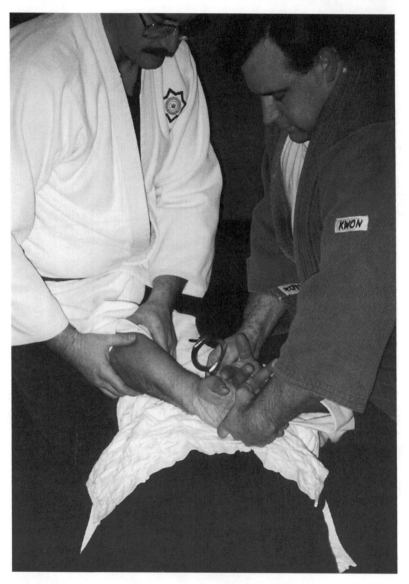

Figure 46. Officer #1 then brings second wrist around for cuffing.

Common Mistakes When Restraining Suspects

The following are common mistakes made by law enforcement officers when restraining and cuffing suspects. They were taught to the author by officer Don Gulla.

1) Not controlling the suspect before cuffing. You must control the suspect before you even take your cuffs out.
2) Not using appropriate counterjoint technique to control.
3) Searching a suspect before cuffing him. During the search the suspect could strike, grab a hidden weapon, or go for the officer's gun.
4) Using necessary force too late to prevent injury to officer and suspect.
5) Not telling the suspect what you want him to do. Suspect may comply if he knows exactly what you want him to do.
6) Not using your weight and good technique to wear the suspect down to allow you to cuff him.
7) Not knowing how or when to rest in a safe position when an arrest situation will take the officer to total exhaustion.

PAROLE/PROBATION SITUATIONS

Certain steps must be taken before physical contact is made with a parole or probation violator. The subject's size and physical attributes, history (including any threats made in the past), potential risk of violence, and mental state are taken into consideration. In some situations weapons are always carried; in others they need to be requested and approved. In either case, the safety of the officer comes first. In all cases, liability of the department and safety of the subject are definite concerns. Even after a plan has been constructed, the team must always be aware that the situation could explode upon contact.

The following is a basic self-defense and control plan used by parole and probation officers. This plan will vary, depending on how volatile the situation is:

1) Preplanning and determining need for police backup
2) Contact and verbal defusing
3) Voice commands
4) Basic stance
5) Team positioning
6) Techniques to escape from grabs, evade or block an attack, and avoid injury
7) Strikes to stun, use of debilitating spray, or escape and regroup
8) Physical control and cuffing
9) Arrest and transport
10) Debriefing

PUBLIC SERVANTS

People whose profession puts them in contact with the general public should take some type of class on dealing with hostile behavior. Taxi drivers, parking meter patrol, emergency ward personnel, teachers, bus drivers, cashiers, bartenders, police officers, mental health professionals, community center staff, park personnel, lifeguards, nurses—anybody who deals with the public never knows what type of person he or she is dealing with. It can be dangerous being forced to confront, defuse, or restrain drunks, criminals, the mentally ill, irrational or emotionally charged people, and drug-crazed individuals.

The following information is based on an interview with Darryl Briggs, a transit bus operator for 18 years who has taken self-defense training with the author. Although the specifics will vary from job to job, the general lessons can apply to all people who work in public service occupations.

Defusing hostile behavior begins before an act actually takes place. Passive measures include posting warning signs stating that plainclothes police ride the bus as well as signs describing acceptable and unacceptable conduct.

If a problem develops with a passenger, the driver can radio the dispatcher with a description of the unruly individual. He should try to determine what is motivating the hostile person's anger. To defuse the situation, the driver should allow the person to let out some steam, within reasonable limits.

Drivers should understand that for some people, the bus is their only method of transportation and that most would not jeopardize losing this privilege. Free ride coupons can be used as incentives or as a negotiation tool.

Modern buses are equipped with an emergency button. When this button is pushed, a signal goes directly to a crisis center, which dispatches help to the driver. For buses that do not contain secret alarms, a phone inside the bus can be used. The calls can be monitored by a supervisor and/or law enforcement. A tracking device is mounted on the bus so that headquarters can locate it immediately.

Safety of the driver and passengers is the top priority. Physical self-defense tactics taught to drivers consist of shouting, blocking, and kicking from a seated position. The basic intervention procedure for the transit bus driver is as follows:

1) Use verbal warnings and/or call dispatch.
2) Monitor behavior for signs of escalation.
3) Attempt to defuse the situation. Use calm, nonthreatening voice.
4) Use silent crisis button or coach phone to alert dispatch and/or police.
5) Stop the bus so the tracking system can get a fix on the location of the bus.
6) Open the doors and provide an opportunity for the subject to leave the bus, or wait for law enforcement.
7) Get a good description of the subject and determine which way he went.
8) Evacuate the bus if necessary.

CIVILIANS: THE S.A.F.E. SYSTEM

S.A.F.E. is a self-protection system created by the author as part of a violence prevention program called Protecting Angel. The Protecting Angel program is divided into youth and adult sections. The youth program teaches positive thinking and appropriate behavior, making the right choices, respecting yourself and authority, antigang and antidrug messages, and basic self-defense. The adult program centers on the S.A.F.E. system, which deals with defusing or managing assaultive behavior and a basic step-by-step approach to self-defense.

S.A.F.E. is an acronym that stands for the four basic self-defense elements of the system: get to a <u>safe</u> zone; <u>attack</u> your assailant; <u>floor</u> your assailant; <u>escape</u> to safety.

Safe zone. Figures 47 and 48 show a person stepping off at an angle in order to decrease the chance of injury, increase the advantage to deliver a self-defense technique, or absorb the attack if unable to evade or block it.

Figure 47

Figure 48

Attack your assailant. It is not important *how* you deliver a self-defense strike; however it is important *where* you strike. Yao Mun Nomad, a martial art system created by the author, has a drill called the "Breakdown." It is based on the principles of striking or kicking areas of the head, body, and legs that control vision, breathing, and mobility. The eyes, temple, throat, base of skull, kidneys, upper rib cage, and knees are the basic strike zones.

NOTE: The above techniques may involve the use of potentially deadly force. They are not recommended for professional restraint situations; they would be used *only* in life-threatening situations. The author, his agents, representatives, and associates are not responsible for the use or misuse of this information in training or any actual self-defense application. It is highly recommended that you participate in an official workshop conducted by the author or other qualified instructor prior to attempting *any* of the physical or verbal techniques described in this book.

Floor your assailant. By striking targets that control vision, breathing, and mobility, you immobilize the aggressor long enough for you to take him to the floor with sweeping, tripping, or throwing techniques.

Escape to safety. Once you have immobilized and floored your assailant, flee to safety.

ATTRACTING ATTENTION AND
USING THE ENVIRONMENT

Criminals, attackers, and others who may be doing something illegal do not want an audience, so in a bad situation one of the best things to do is attract attention. This means make as much noise as possible when being attacked.

There are pros and cons to screaming the word "help." Some say that many people do not want to get involved in crimes in progress and will not respond to a cry for help. Because much crime is gang or drug related, people are afraid to get involved for fear of retaliation from criminals. Therefore, another option is to scream out, "Fire! Fire!" Almost everyone will come out to see where the fire is.

If you think you are going to be attacked, put distance and objects between you and the attacker. Use anything in your environment to accomplish this goal. Force the attacker to go around or over something before he can make contact with you. Using a car to put distance between you and the attacker is a good example. Doing this will provide you with valuable seconds with which to escape.

Improvised weapons can be used to distract an attacker. Examples include throwing dirt or water into an assailant's face and following up with a restraining hold, self-defense tactic, or escape, or grabbing anything nearby for use as a weapon. Be creative and consider anything as a potential weapon. Figure 49 shows a woman using her Daytimer to deflect a strike. Figure 50

Figure 49

shows a field case-worker throwing her jacket into the face of an assaultive subject, buying her valuable seconds to flee to safety.

Figure 50

CHAPTER 7

LEGAL ISSUES

Balancing use of force with liability issues is important when dealing with any hands-on restraining of a subject. As stated before, the success of the team depends upon its ability to accomplish the objective without violating the rights of the subject, avoiding injury to the subject, and avoiding injury to the team, all while keeping in mind potential liability concerns of the agency you represent.

NOTE: The author is not an attorney. The following information is for general reference purposes only and is not intended to be legal advice. Consult an attorney and/or your local law enforcement agency and research the laws in your jurisdiction.

USE OF FORCE

In *Barron's Law Dictionary*, Third Edition, by Steven H. Giffs, "force" is defined as physical acts or threat of physical acts intentionally used to do an act or to commit a crime. It further breaks it down into "deadly force" and "unlawful force." The first type deals with force and great bodily harm; the second deals with tort law and force without the consent of the person at whom the force was directed.

In the definition of deadly force, a reference is made to the doctrine of "self-defense," which relates to the use of deadly force to repel deadly force. The use of unlawful force is referred to as "battery." The least amount of touching on a person could be looked upon as battery. An assault could be described as an unauthorized act that causes a person to have fear of imminent harmful or offensive contact. Touching could include any part of the body or anything attached to the body. The fear of offensive contact and the actual touching could be looked upon as "assault and battery."

My advice to a professional is to *not* make physical contact with anyone unless it is vital to your immediate safety or the safety of others. If you have a specialized team to handle this type of situation, activate it. Mental health hospitals, for example, usually have a response team that's trained to deal with situations that are potentially harmful to the patient or others. Also, never intervene with a person of the opposite sex without having another professional present, preferably of the same sex as the subject.

ARREST

Barron's Law Dictionary defines "arrest" as depriving a person of his liberty by legal authority. When you detain, hold, or arrest someone, you are in a sense depriving that person of liberty, which can be looked upon as performing an unauthorized restraint. When I worked in a mental health facility, we needed to obtain a doctor's order before placing a subject into locked seclusion or applying restraint devices that limited the subject's movement. When it comes to detaining someone, performing an arrest, or holding someone against his will, you could be charged with false arrest, false imprisonment, or assault and battery.

My advice is to let the police perform an arrest. If you as a professional are contemplating whether to restrain a hostile subject, first try implementing a show of force or activating a professional assault response team if you have one. If not, call 911. The private citizen is better off taking a good description of the perpetrator, documenting everything possible, contacting the police immediately, and not attempting a citizen's arrest.

REVISED CODE OF WASHINGTON (RCW)

The following are Washington state laws on self-defense, assault, homicide, and insanity. I am only using Washington as an example; you should research laws that govern your state or seek legal advice from an attorney in your area.

If you are under the jurisdiction of Washington state, as an extra precaution I advise you to seek legal counsel prior to interpreting the RCW as reprinted below. I am not an attorney or law enforcement officer, nor am I providing legal advice by reprinting laws that were current as of this book's publication date.

Washington Criminal Code
Chapter 9a.16 RCW
Defenses

RCW 9A.16.010 Definitions.

In this chapter, unless a different meaning is plainly required:

(1) "Necessary" means that no reasonably effective alternative to the use of force appeared to exist and that the amount of force used was reasonable to effect the lawful purpose intended.

(2) "Deadly force" means the intentional application of force through the use of firearms or any other means reasonably likely to cause death or serious physical injury. [1986 c 209 § 1; 1975 1st ex.s. c 260 § 9A.16.010.]

RCW 9A.16.020 Use of force—When lawful.

The use, attempt, or offer to use force upon or toward the person of another is not unlawful in the following cases:

(1) Whenever necessarily used by a public officer in the per-

formance of a legal duty, or a person assisting the officer and acting under the officer's direction;

(2) Whenever necessarily used by a person arresting one who has committed a felony and delivering him or her to a public officer competent to receive him or her into custody;

(3) Whenever used by a party about to be injured, or by another lawfully aiding him or her, in preventing or attempting to prevent an offense against his or her person, or a malicious trespass, or other malicious interference with real or personal property lawfully in his or her possession, in case the force is not more than is necessary;

(4) Whenever reasonably used by a person to detain someone who enters or remains unlawfully in a building or on real property lawfully in the possession of such person, so long as such detention is reasonable in duration and manner to investigate the reason for the detained person's presence on the premises, and so long as the premises in question did not reasonably appear to be intended to be open to members of the public;

(5) Whenever used by a carrier of passengers or the carrier's authorized agent or servant, or other person assisting him at his request in expelling from a carriage, railway car, vessel, or other vehicle, a passenger who refuses to obey a lawful and reasonable regulation prescribed for the conduct of passengers, if such vehicle has first been stopped and the force used is not more than is necessary to expel the offender with reasonable regard to the offender's personal safety;

(6) Whenever used by any person to prevent a mentally ill, mentally incompetent, or mentally disabled person from committing an act dangerous to any person, or in enforcing necessary restraint for the protection or restoration to health of the person, during such period only as is necessary to obtain legal authority for the restraint or custody of the person. [1986 c 149 § 2; 1979 ex.s. c 244 § 7; 1977 ex.s. c 80 § 13; 1975 1st ex.s. c 260 § 9A.16.020.]

NOTES:

Effective date—1979 ex.s. c 244: See RCW 9A.44.902.

Purpose—Intent—Severability—1977 ex.s. c 80: See notes following RCW 4.16.190.

RCW 9A.16.030 Homicide—When excusable.
Homicide is excusable when committed by accident or misfortune in doing any lawful act by lawful means, without criminal negligence, or without any unlawful intent. [1979 ex.s. c 244 § 8; 1975 1st ex.s. c 260 § 9A.16.030.]
NOTES:
Effective date—1979 ex.s. c 244: See RCW 9A.44.902

RCW 9A.16.040 Justifiable homicide or use of deadly force by public officer, peace officer, person aiding.
(1) Homicide or the use of deadly force is justifiable in the following cases:
(a) When a public officer is acting in obedience to the judgment of a competent court; or
(b) When necessarily used by a peace officer to overcome actual resistance to the execution of the legal process, mandate, or order of a court or officer, or in the discharge of a legal duty.
(c) When necessarily used by a peace officer or person acting under the officer's command and in the officer's aid:
(i) To arrest or apprehend a person who the officer reasonably believes has committed, has attempted to commit, is committing, or is attempting to commit a felony;
(ii) To prevent the escape of a person from a federal or state correctional facility or in retaking a person who escapes from such a facility; or
(iii) To prevent the escape of a person from a county or city jail or holding facility if the person has been arrested for, charged with, or convicted of a felony; or
(iv) To lawfully suppress a riot if the actor or another participant is armed with a deadly weapon.
(2) In considering whether to use deadly force under subsection (1)(c) of this section, to arrest or apprehend any person for the

commission of any crime, the peace officer must have probable cause to believe that the suspect, if not apprehended, poses a threat of serious physical harm to the officer or a threat of serious physical harm to others. Among the circumstances which may be considered by peace officers as a "threat of serious physical harm" are the following:

(a) The suspect threatens a peace officer with a weapon or displays a weapon in a manner that could reasonably be construed as threatening; or

(b) There is probable cause to believe that the suspect has committed any crime involving the infliction or threatened infliction of serious physical harm. Under these circumstances deadly force may also be used if necessary to prevent escape from the officer, where, if feasible, some warning is given.

(3) A public officer or peace officer shall not be held criminally liable for using deadly force without malice and with a good faith belief that such act is justifiable pursuant to this section.

(4) This section shall not be construed as:

(a) Affecting the permissible use of force by a person acting under the authority of RCW 9A.16.020 or 9A.16.050; or

(b) Preventing a law enforcement agency from adopting standards pertaining to its use of deadly force that are more restrictive than this section. [1986 c 209 § 2; 1975 1st ex.s. c 260 § 9A.16.040.]

NOTES:

Legislative recognition: "The legislature recognizes that RCW 9A.16.040 establishes a dual standard with respect to the use of deadly force by peace officers and private citizens, and further recognizes that private citizens' permissible use of deadly force under the authority of RCW 9.01.200, 9A.16.020, or 9A.16.050 is not restricted and remains broader than the limitations imposed on peace officers." [1986 c 209 § 3.]

RCW 9A.16.050 *Homicide—By other person—When justifiable.* Homicide is also justifiable when committed either:

(1) In the lawful defense of the slayer, or his or her husband, wife, parent, child, brother, or sister, or of any other person in his presence or company, when there is reasonable ground to apprehend a design on the part of the person slain to commit a felony or to do some great personal injury to the slayer or to any such person, and there is imminent danger of such design being accomplished; or

(2) In the actual resistance of an attempt to commit a felony upon the slayer, in his presence, or upon or in a dwelling, or other place of abode, in which he is. [1975 1st ex.s. c 260 § 9A.16.050.]

RCW 9A.16.060 Duress.

(1) In any prosecution for a crime, it is a defense that:

(a) The actor participated in the crime under compulsion by another who by threat or use of force created an apprehension in the mind of the actor that in case of refusal he or another would be liable to immediate death or immediate grievous bodily injury; and

(b) That such apprehension was reasonable upon the part of the actor; and

(c) That the actor would not have participated in the crime except for the duress involved.

(2) The defense of duress is not available if the crime charged is murder or manslaughter.

(3) The defense of duress is not available if the actor intentionally or recklessly places himself in a situation in which it is probable that he will be subject to duress.

(4) The defense of duress is not established solely by a showing that a married person acted on the command of his or her spouse. [1975 1st ex.s. c 260 § 9A.16.060.]

RCW 9A.16.070 Entrapment.

(1) In any prosecution for a crime, it is a defense that:

(a) The criminal design originated in the mind of law enforcement officials, or any person acting under his direction, and

(b) The actor was lured or induced to commit a crime which the actor had not otherwise intended to commit.

(2) The defense of entrapment is not established by a showing only that law enforcement officials merely afforded the actor an opportunity to commit a crime. [1975 1st ex.s. c 260 § 9A.16.070.]

RCW 9A.16.080 Action for being detained on mercantile establishment premises for investigation—"Reasonable grounds" as defense.

In any criminal action brought by reason of any person having been detained on or in the immediate vicinity of the premises of a mercantile establishment for the purpose of investigation or questioning as to the ownership of any merchandise, it shall be a defense of such action that the person was detained in a reasonable manner and for not more than a reasonable time to permit such investigation or questioning by a peace officer, by the owner of the mercantile establishment, or by the owner's authorized employee or agent, and that such peace officer, owner, employee, or agent had reasonable grounds to believe that the person so detained was committing or attempting to commit theft or shoplifting on such premises of such merchandise. As used in this section, "reasonable grounds" shall include, but not be limited to, knowledge that a person has concealed possession of unpurchased merchandise of a mercantile establishment, and a "reasonable time" shall mean the time necessary to permit the person detained to make a statement or to refuse to make a statement, and the time necessary to examine employees and records of the mercantile establishment relative to the ownership of the merchandise. [1975 1st ex.s. c 260 § 9A.16.080.]

RCW 9A.16.090 Intoxication.

No act committed by a person while in a state of voluntary intoxication shall be deemed less criminal by reason of his condition, but whenever the actual existence of any particular mental state is a necessary element to constitute a particular species or degree of crime, the fact of his intoxication may be taken into consideration in determining such mental state. [1975 1st ex.s. c 260 § 9A.16.090.]

RCW 9A.16.100 *Use of force on children—Policy—Actions presumed unreasonable.*

It is the policy of this state to protect children from assault and abuse and to encourage parents, teachers, and authorized agents to use methods of correction and restraint of children that are not dangerous to the children. However, the physical discipline of a child is not unlawful when it is reasonable and moderate and is inflicted by a parent, teacher, or guardian for purposes of restraining or correcting the child. Any use of force on a child by any other person is unlawful unless it is reasonable and moderate and is authorized in advance by the child's parent or guardian for purposes of restraining or correcting the child.

The following actions are presumed unreasonable when used to correct or restrain a child:

(1) Throwing, kicking, burning, or cutting a child;

(2) striking a child with a closed fist;

(3) shaking a child under age three;

(4) interfering with a child's breathing;

(5) threatening a child with a deadly weapon; or

(6) doing any other act that is likely to cause and which does cause bodily harm greater than transient pain or minor temporary marks.

The age, size, and condition of the child and the location of the injury shall be considered when determining whether the bodily harm is reasonable or moderate. This list is illustrative of unreasonable actions and is not intended to be exclusive. [1986 c 149 § 1.]

RCW 9A.16.110 *Defending against violent crime—Reimbursement.*

(1) No person in the state shall be placed in legal jeopardy of any kind whatsoever for protecting by any reasonable means neces-

sary, himself or herself, his or her family, or his or her real or property, or for coming to the aid of another who is in imminent danger of or the victim of assault, robbery, kidnapping, arson, burglary, rape, murder, or any other violent crime as defined in RCW 9.94A.030.

(2) When a person charged with a crime listed in subsection (1) of this section is found not guilty by reason of self-defense, the state of Washington shall reimburse the defendant for all reasonable costs, including loss of time, legal fees incurred, and other expenses involved in his or her defense. This reimbursement is not an independent cause of action. To award these reasonable costs the trier of fact must find that the defendant's claim of self-defense was sustained by a preponderance of the evidence. If the trier of fact makes a determination of self-defense, the judge shall determine the amount of the award.

(3) Notwithstanding a finding that a defendant's actions were justified by self-defense, if the trier of fact also determines that the defendant was engaged in criminal conduct substantially related to the events giving rise to the charges filed against the defendant the judge may deny or reduce the amount of the award. In determining the amount of the award, the judge shall also consider the seriousness of the initial criminal conduct. Nothing in this section precludes the legislature from using the sundry claims process to grant an award where none was granted under this section or to grant a higher award than one granted under this section.

(4) Whenever the issue of self-defense under this section is decided by a judge, the judge shall consider the same questions as must be answered in the special verdict under subsection (4) [(5)] of this section.

(5) Whenever the issue of self-defense under this section has been submitted to a jury, and the jury has found the defendant not guilty, the court shall instruct the jury to return a special verdict in substantially the following form:

[answer yes or no]

1. Was the finding of not guilty based upon self-defense?

2. If your answer to question 1 is no, do not answer the remaining questions.

3. If your answer to question 1 is yes, was the defendant:

    a. Protecting himself or herself?

    b. Protecting his or her family?

    c. Protecting his or her property?

    d. Coming to the aid of another who was in imminent danger of a heinous crime?

    e. Coming to the aid of another who was the victim of a heinous crime?

    f. Engaged in criminal conduct substantially related to the events giving rise to the crime with which the defendant is charged?

[1995 c 44 § 1; 1989 c 94 § 1; 1977 ex.s. c 206 § 8. Formerly RCW 9.01.200.]

NOTES:

Use of deadly force—Legislative recognition: See note following RCW 9A.16.040.

Washington Criminal Code
Chapter 9a.12 RCW
Insanity

RCW 9A.12.010 *Insanity.*

To establish the defense of insanity, it must be shown that:

(1) At the time of the commission of the offense, as a result of mental disease or defect, the mind of the actor was affected to such an extent that:

    (a) He was unable to perceive the nature and quality of the act with which he is charged; or

    (b) He was unable to tell right from wrong with reference to the particular act charged.

(2) The defense of insanity must be established by a preponderance of the evidence. [1975 1st ex.s. c 260 § 9A.12.010.]

Washington Criminal Code
Chapter 9a.36 RCW
Assault—Physical Harm

For the sake of brevity, I will only present the laws for assault, reckless endangerment, harassment, coercion, custodial assault, assault of a child, and domestic violence. If any other sections of this code are of interest to you, go to the Washington state home page on the Internet and search for RCW—Revised Code of Washington (or the applicable page on your home state's Web site).

RCW 9A.36.011 Assault in the first degree.

(1) A person is guilty of assault in the first degree if he or she, with intent to inflict great bodily harm:

(a) Assaults another with a firearm or any deadly weapon or by any force or means likely to produce great bodily harm or death; or

(b) Administers, exposes, or transmits to or causes to be taken by another, poison, the human immunodeficiency virus as defined in chapter 70.24 RCW, or any other destructive or noxious substance; or

(c) Assaults another and inflicts great bodily harm.

(2) Assault in the first degree is a class A felony. [1997 c 196 § 1; 1986 c 257 § 4.]

NOTES:

Severability—1986 c 257: See note following RCW 9A.56.010.

Effective date—1986 c 257 §§ 3-10: See note following RCW 9A.04.110.

RCW 9A.36.021 Assault in the second degree.

(1) A person is guilty of assault in the second degree if he or she, under circumstances not amounting to assault in the first degree:

(a) Intentionally assaults another and thereby recklessly inflicts substantial bodily harm; or

(b) Intentionally and unlawfully causes substantial bodily harm to an unborn child by intentionally and unlawfully inflicting any injury upon the mother of such child; or

(c) Assaults another with a deadly weapon; or

(d) With intent to inflict bodily harm, administers to or causes to be taken by another, poison or any other destructive or noxious substance; or

(e) With intent to commit a felony, assaults another; or

(f) Knowingly inflicts bodily harm which by design causes such pain or agony as to be the equivalent of that produced by torture.

(2) Assault in the second degree is a class B felony. [1997 c 196 § 2. Prior: 1988 c 266 § 2; 1988 c 206 § 916; 1988 c 158 § 2; 1987 c 324 § 2; 1986 c 257 § 5.]

NOTES:

Effective date—1988 c 266: "This act is necessary for the immediate preservation of the public peace, health, and safety, the support of the state government and its existing public institutions, and shall take effect July 1, 1988." [1988 c 266 § 3.]

Effective date—1988 c 206 §§ 916, 917: "Sections 916 and 917 of this act shall take effect July 1, 1988." [1988 c 206 § 922.]

Severability—1988 c 206: See RCW 70.24.900.

Effective date—1988 c 158: See note following RCW 9A.04.110.

Effective date—1987 c 324: See note following RCW 9A.04.110.

Severability—1986 c 257: See note following RCW 9A.56.010.

Effective date—1986 c 257 §§ 3-10: See note following RCW 9A.04.110.

RCW 9A.36.031 Assault in the third degree.

(1) A person is guilty of assault in the third degree if he or she, under circumstances not amounting to assault in the first or second degree:

(a) With intent to prevent or resist the execution of any

lawful process or mandate of any court officer or the lawful apprehension or detention of himself or another person, assaults another; or

(b) Assaults a person employed as a transit operator or driver by a public or private transit company while that person is performing his or her official duties at the time of the assault; or

(c) Assaults a school bus driver employed by a school district or a private company under contract for transportation services with a school district while the driver is performing his or her official duties at the time of the assault; or

(d) With criminal negligence, causes bodily harm to another person by means of a weapon or other instrument or thing likely to produce bodily harm; or

(e) Assaults a fire fighter or other employee of a fire department, county fire marshal's office, county fire prevention bureau, or fire protection district who was performing his or her official duties at the time of the assault; or

(f) With criminal negligence, causes bodily harm accompanied by substantial pain that extends for a period sufficient to cause considerable suffering; or

(g) Assaults a law enforcement officer or other employee of a law enforcement agency who was performing his or her official duties at the time of the assault; or

(h) Assaults a nurse, physician, or health care provider who was performing his or her nursing or health care duties at the time of the assault. For purposes of this subsection: "Nurse" means a person licensed under chapter 18.79 RCW; "physician" means a person licensed under chapter 18.57 or 18.71 RCW; and "health care provider" means a person certified under chapter 18.71 or 18.73 RCW who performs emergency medical services or a person regulated under Title 18 RCW and employed by, or contracting with, a hospital licensed under chapter 70.41 RCW.

(2) Assault in the third degree is a class C felony. [1998 c 94 § 1; 1997 c 172 § 1; 1996 c 266 § 1; 1990 c 236 § 1; 1989 c 169 § 1; 1988 c 158 § 3; 1986 c 257 § 6.]

NOTES:

Effective date—1988 c 158: See note following RCW
9A.04.110.

Severability—1986 c 257: See note following RCW 9A.56.010.

Effective date—1986 c 257 §§ 3-10: See note following RCW
9A.04.110.

RCW 9A.36.041 Assault in the fourth degree.

(1) A person is guilty of assault in the fourth degree if, under
circumstances not amounting to assault in the first, second, or
third degree, or custodial assault, he or she assaults another.

(2) Assault in the fourth degree is a gross misdemeanor. [1987
c 188 § 2; 1986 c 257 § 7.]

NOTES:

Effective date—1986 c 257 §§ 3-10: See note following RCW
9A.04.110.

Effective date—1987 c 188: See note following RCW
9A.36.100.

Severability—1986 c 257: See note following RCW 9A.56.010.

RCW 9A.36.050 Reckless endangerment.

(1) A person is guilty of reckless endangerment when he or she
recklessly engages in conduct not amounting to drive-by shooting
but that creates a substantial risk of death or serious physical injury
to another person.

(2) Reckless endangerment is a gross misdemeanor. [1997 c
338 § 45; 1989 c 271 § 110; 1975 1st ex.s. c 260 § 9A.36.050.]

NOTES:

Finding—Evaluation—Report—1997 c 338: See note following RCW 13.40.0357.

Severability—Effective dates—1997 c 338: See notes following
RCW 5.60.060.

Finding—Intent—1989 c 271 §§ 102, 109, and 110: "The legislature finds that increased trafficking in illegal drugs has
increased the likelihood of "drive-by shootings." It is the intent of

the legislature in sections 102, 109, and 110 of this act to catego-
rize such reckless and criminal activity into a separate crime and
to provide for an appropriate punishment." [1989 c 271 § 108.]
"Sections 102, 109, and 110 of this act" consist of the enactment
of RCW 9A.36.045 and the 1989 c 271 amendments to RCW
9.94A.320 and 9A.36.050.
　　Application—1989 c 271 §§ 101-111: See note following
RCW 9.94A.310.
　　Severability—1989 c 271: See note following RCW 9.94A.310.
　　Criminal history and driving record: RCW 46.61.513.

RCW 9A.36.070 Coercion.
　(1) A person is guilty of coercion if by use of a threat he com-
pels or induces a person to engage in conduct which the latter has
a legal right to abstain from, or to abstain from conduct which he
has a legal right to engage in.
　(2) "Threat" as used in this section means:
　　(a) To communicate, directly or indirectly, the intent
immediately to use force against any person who is present at the
time; or
　　(b) Threats as defined in RCW 9A.04.110(25)(a), (b), or
(c).
　(3) Coercion is a gross misdemeanor. [1975 1st ex.s. c 260 §
9A.36.070.]

　RCW 9A.36.078 Malicious harassment—Finding.
　The legislature finds that crimes and threats against persons
because of his race, color, religion, ancestry, national origin, gender, sexual orientation, or mental, physical, or sensory handicaps
are serious and increasing. The legislature also finds that crimes
and threats are often directed against interracial couples and their
children or couples of mixed religions, colors, ancestries, or
national origins because of bias and bigotry against the race, color,
religion, ancestry, or national origin of one person in the couple or
family. The legislature finds that the state interest in preventing

crimes and threats motivated by bigotry and bias goes beyond the state interest in preventing other felonies or misdemeanors such as criminal trespass, malicious mischief, assault, or other crimes that are not motivated by hatred, bigotry, and bias, and that prosecution of those other crimes inadequately protects citizens from crimes and threats motivated by bigotry and bias. Therefore, the legislature finds that protection of those citizens from threats of harm due to bias and bigotry is a compelling state interest. The legislature also finds that in many cases, certain discrete words or symbols are used to threaten the victims. Those discrete words or symbols have historically or traditionally been used to connote hatred or threats towards members of the class of which the victim or a member of the victim's family or household is a member. In particular, the legislature finds that cross burnings historically and traditionally have been used to threaten, terrorize, intimidate, and harass African Americans and their families. Cross burnings often preceded lynchings, murders, burning of homes, and other acts of terror. Further, Nazi swastikas historically and traditionally have been used to threaten, terrorize, intimidate, and harass Jewish people and their families. Swastikas symbolize the massive destruction of the Jewish population, commonly known as the holocaust. Therefore, the legislature finds that any person who burns or attempts to burn a cross or displays a swastika on the property of the victim or burns a cross or displays a swastika as part of a series of acts directed towards a particular person, the person's family or household members, or a particular group, knows or reasonably should know that the cross burning or swastika may create a reasonable fear of harm in the mind of the person, the person's family and household members, or the group. The legislature also finds that a hate crime committed against a victim because of the victim's gender may be identified in the same manner that a hate crime committed against a victim of another protected group is identified. Affirmative indications of hatred towards gender as a class is the predominant factor to consider. Other factors to consider include the perpetrator's use of language, slurs, or symbols expressing hatred towards the victim's gender as a class; the severity of the attack including mutilation of the victim's sexual organs; a history of similar attacks against victims of the same gender by the perpetrator or a history of similar incidents in the same area; a lack of provocation; an absence of any other apparent motivation; and common sense. [1993 c 127 § 1.]

NOTES:

Severability—1993 c 127: "If any provision of this act or its application to any person or circumstance is held invalid, the remainder of the act or the application of the provision to other persons or circumstances is not affected." [1993 c 127 § 7.]

RCW 9A.36.080 Malicious harassment—Definition and criminal penalty.

(1) A person is guilty of malicious harassment if he or she maliciously and intentionally commits one of the following acts because of his or her perception of the victim's race, color, religion, ancestry, national origin, gender, sexual orientation, or mental, physical, or sensory handicap:

(a) Causes physical injury to the victim or another person;

(b) Causes physical damage to or destruction of the property of the victim or another person; or

(c) Threatens a specific person or group of persons and places that person, or members of the specific group of persons, in reasonable fear of harm to person or property. The fear must be a fear that a reasonable person would have under all the circumstances. For purposes of this section, a "reasonable person" is a reasonable person who is a member of the victim's race, color, religion, ancestry, national origin, gender, or sexual orientation, or who has the same mental, physical, or sensory handicap as the victim. Words alone do not constitute malicious harassment unless the context or circumstances surrounding the words indicate the words are a threat. Threatening words do not constitute malicious harassment if it is apparent to the victim that the person does not have the ability to carry out the threat.

(2) In any prosecution for malicious harassment, unless evidence exists which explains to the trier of fact's satisfaction that the person did not intend to threaten the victim or victims, the trier of fact may infer that the person intended to threaten a specific victim or group of victims because of the person's perception of the victim's or victims' race, color, religion, ancestry, national origin, gender, sexual orientation, or mental, physical, or sensory handicap if the person commits one of the following acts:

(a) Burns a cross on property of a victim who is or whom the actor perceives to be of African American heritage; or

(b) Defaces property of a victim who is or whom the actor perceives to be of Jewish heritage by defacing the property with a swastika. This subsection only applies to the creation of a reasonable inference for evidentiary purposes. This subsection does not restrict the state's ability to prosecute a person under subsection (1) of this section when the facts of a particular case do not fall within (a) or (b) of this subsection.

(3) It is not a defense that the accused was mistaken that the victim was a member of a certain race, color, religion, ancestry, national origin, gender, or sexual orientation, or had a mental, physical, or sensory handicap.

(4) Evidence of expressions or associations of the accused may not be introduced as substantive evidence at trial unless the evidence specifically relates to the crime charged. Nothing in this chapter shall affect the rules of evidence governing impeachment of a witness.

(5) Every person who commits another crime during the commission of a crime under this section may be punished and prosecuted for the other crime separately.

(6) "Sexual orientation" for the purposes of this section means heterosexuality, homosexuality, or bisexuality.

(7) Malicious harassment is a class C felony.

(8) The penalties provided in this section for malicious harassment do not preclude the victims from seeking any other remedies otherwise available under law.

(9) Nothing in this section confers or expands any civil rights or protections to any group or class identified under this section, beyond those rights or protections that exist under the federal or state Constitution or the civil laws of the state of Washington. [1993 c 127 § 2; 1989 c 95 § 1; 1984 c 268 § 1; 1981
 c 267 § 1.]
 NOTES:
 Severability—1993 c 127: See note following RCW 9A.36.078.
 Construction—1989 c 95: "The provisions of this act shall be liberally construed in order to effectuate its purpose." [1989 c 95 § 3.]
 Severability—1989 c 95: "If any provision of this act or its application to any person or circumstance is held invalid, the remainder of the act or the application of the provision to other persons or circumstances is not affected." [1989 c 95 § 4.]
Harassment: Chapters 9A.46 and 10.14 RCW.

RCW 9A.36.083 Malicious harassment—Civil action.
 In addition to the criminal penalty provided in RCW 9A.36.080 for committing a crime of malicious harassment, the victim may bring a civil cause of action for malicious harassment against the harasser. A person may be liable to the victim of malicious harassment for actual damages, punitive damages of up to ten thousand dollars, and reasonable attorneys' fees and costs incurred in bringing the action. [1993 c 127 § 3.]
 NOTES:
 Severability—1993 c 127: See note following RCW 9A.36.078.

RCW 9A.36.100 Custodial assault.
 (1) A person is guilty of custodial assault if that person is not guilty of an assault in the first or second degree and where the person:
  (a) Assaults a full or part-time staff member or volunteer, any educational personnel, any personal service provider, or any vendor or agent thereof at any juvenile corrections institution or

local juvenile detention facilities who was performing official duties at the time of the assault;

(b) Assaults a full or part-time staff member or volunteer, any educational personnel, any personal service provider, or any vendor or agent thereof at any adult corrections institution or local adult detention facilities who was performing official duties at the time of the assault;

(c)   (i) Assaults a full or part-time community correction officer while the officer is performing official duties; or

(ii) Assaults any other full or part-time employee who is employed in a community corrections office while the employee is performing official duties; or

(d) Assaults any volunteer who was assisting a person described in (c) of this subsection at the time of the assault.

(2) Custodial assault is a class C felony. [1988 c 151 § 1; 1987 c 188 § 1.]

NOTES:

Effective date—1987 c 188: "This act is necessary for the immediate preservation of the public peace, health, and safety, the support of the state government and its existing public institutions, and shall take effect July 1, 1987." [1987 c 188 § 3.]

RCW 9A.36.120 *Assault of a child in the first degree.*

(1) A person eighteen years of age or older is guilty of the crime of assault of a child in the first degree if the child is under the age of thirteen and the person:

(a) Commits the crime of assault in the first degree, as defined in RCW 9A.36.011, against the child; or

(b) Intentionally assaults the child and either:

(i) Recklessly inflicts great bodily harm; or

(ii) Causes substantial bodily harm, and the person has previously engaged in a pattern or practice either of

(A) assaulting the child which has resulted in bodily harm that is greater than transient physical pain or minor temporary marks, or

(B) causing the child physical pain or
agony that is equivalent to that produced by torture.
(2) Assault of a child in the first degree is a class A felony.
[1992 c 145 § 1.]

RCW 9A.36.130 *Assault of a child in the second degree.*
(1) A person eighteen years of age or older is guilty of the
crime of assault of a child in the second degree if the child is
under the age of thirteen and the person:
(a) Commits the crime of assault in the second degree, as
defined in RCW 9A.36.021, against a child; or
(b) Intentionally assaults the child and causes bodily
harm that is greater than transient physical pain or minor temporary marks, and the person has previously engaged in a pattern or
practice either of
(i) assaulting the child which has resulted in bodily
harm that is greater than transient pain or minor temporary marks, or
(ii) causing the child physical pain or agony that is
equivalent to that produced by torture.
(2) Assault of a child in the second degree is a class B felony.
[1992 c 145 § 2.]

RCW 9A.36.140 *Assault of a child in the third degree.*
(1) A person eighteen years of age or older is guilty of the
crime of assault of a child in the third degree if the child is
under the age of thirteen and the person commits the crime of
assault in the third degree as defined in RCW 9A.36.031(1)(d) or
(f) against the child.
(2) Assault of a child in the third degree is a class C felony.
[1992 c 145 § 3.]

RCW 9A.36.150 *Interfering with the reporting of domestic
violence.*
(1) A person commits the crime of interfering with the reporting of domestic violence if the person:

(a) Commits a crime of domestic violence, as defined in RCW 10.99.020; and

(b) Prevents or attempts to prevent the victim of or a witness to that domestic violence crime from calling a 911 emergency communication system, obtaining medical assistance, or making a report to any law enforcement official.

(2) Commission of a crime of domestic violence under subsection (1) of this section is a necessary element of the crime of interfering with the reporting of domestic violence.

(3) Interference with the reporting of domestic violence is a gross misdemeanor. [1996 c 248 § 3.]

Washington Criminal Code
Chapter 9a.32 RCW
Homicide

RCW 9A.32.010 Homicide defined.

Homicide is the killing of a human being by the act, procurement, or omission of another, death occurring at any time, and is either

(1) murder,

(2) homicide by abuse,

(3) manslaughter,

(4) excusable homicide, or

(5) justifiable homicide. [1997 c 196 § 3; 1987 c 187 § 2; 1983 c 10 § 1; 1975 1st ex.s. c 260 § 9A.32.010.]

NOTES:

Excusable homicide: RCW 9A.16.030.

Justifiable homicide: RCW 9A.16.040 and 9A.16.050.

RCW 9A.32.020 Premeditation—Limitations.

(1) As used in this chapter, the premeditation required in order to support a conviction of the crime of murder in the first degree must involve more than a moment in point of time.

(2) Nothing contained in this chapter shall affect RCW 46.61.520. [1975 1st ex.s. c 260 § 9A.32.020.]

RCW 9A.32.030 *Murder in the first degree.*

(1) A person is guilty of murder in the first degree when:

(a) With a premeditated intent to cause the death of another person, he or she causes the death of such person or of a third person; or

(b) Under circumstances manifesting an extreme indifference to human life, he or she engages in conduct which creates a grave risk of death to any person, and thereby causes the death of a person; or

(c) He or she commits or attempts to commit the crime of either

(1) robbery in the first or second degree,

(2) rape in the first or second degree,

(3) burglary in the first degree,

(4) arson in the first or second degree, or

(5) kidnapping in the first or second degree, and in the course of or in furtherance of such crime or in immediate flight therefrom, he or she, or another participant, causes the death of a person other than one of the participants: Except that in any prosecution under this subdivision (1)(c) in which the defendant was not the only participant in the underlying crime, if established by the defendant by a preponderance of the evidence, it is a defense that the defendant:

(i) Did not commit the homicidal act or in any way solicit, request, command, importune, cause, or aid the commission thereof; and

(ii) Was not armed with a deadly weapon, or any instrument, article, or substance readily capable of causing death or serious physical injury; and

(iii) Had no reasonable grounds to believe that any other participant was armed with such a weapon, instrument, article, or substance; and

(iv) Had no reasonable grounds to believe that any other participant intended to engage in conduct likely to result in death or serious physical injury.

(2) Murder in the first degree is a class A felony. [1990 c 200 § 1; 1975-'76 2nd ex.s. c 38 § 3; 1975 1st ex.s. c 260 § 9A.32.030.]
NOTES:
Effective date—Severability—1975-'76 2nd ex.s. c 38: See NOTES following RCW 9A.08.020.

RCW 9A.32.040 Murder in the first degree—Sentence.
Notwithstanding RCW 9A.32.030(2), any person convicted of the crime of murder in the first degree shall be sentenced to life imprisonment. [1982 c 10 § 2. Prior: (1) 1981 c 138 § 21; 1977 ex.s. c 206 § 3; 1975 1st ex.s. c 260 § 9A.32.040. (2) 1981 c 136 § 55 repealed by 1982 c 10 § 18.]NOTES:
Severability—1982 c 10: See note following RCW 6.13.080.
Severability—1981 c 138: See RCW 10.95.900.
Effective date—1981 c 136: See RCW 72.09.900.
Capital punishment—Aggravated first degree murder: Chapter 10.95 RCW.

RCW 9A.32.050 Murder in the second degree.
(1) A person is guilty of murder in the second degree when:
(a) With intent to cause the death of another person but without premeditation, he causes the death of such person or of a third person; or
(b) He commits or attempts to commit any felony other than those enumerated in RCW 9A.32.030(1)(c), and, in the course of and in furtherance of such crime or in immediate flight therefrom, he, or another participant, causes the death of a person other than one of the participants; except that in any prosecution under this subdivision (1)(b) in which the defendant was not the only participant in the underlying crime, if established by the defendant by a preponderance of the evidence, it is a defense that the defendant:
(i) Did not commit the homicidal act or in any way solicit, request, command, importune, cause, or aid the commission thereof; and

(ii) Was not armed with a deadly weapon, or any instrument, article, or substance readily capable of causing death or serious physical injury; and

(iii) Had no reasonable grounds to believe that any other participant was armed with such a weapon, instrument, article, or substance; and

(iv) Had no reasonable grounds to believe that any other participant intended to engage in conduct likely to result in death or serious physical injury.

(2) Murder in the second degree is a class A felony. [1975-'76 2nd ex.s. c 38 § 4; 1975 1st ex.s. c 260 § 9A.32.050.]

NOTES:

Effective date—Severability—1975-'76 2nd ex.s. c 38: See NOTES following RCW 9A.08.020.

RCW 9A.32.055 Homicide by abuse.

(1) A person is guilty of homicide by abuse if, under circumstances manifesting an extreme indifference to human life, the person causes the death of a child or person under sixteen years of age, a developmentally disabled person, or a dependent adult, and the person has previously engaged in a pattern or practice of assault or torture of said child, person under sixteen years of age, developmentally disabled person, or dependent person.

(2) As used in this section, "dependent adult" means a person who, because of physical or mental disability, or because of extreme advanced age, is dependent upon another person to provide the basic necessities of life.

(3) Homicide by abuse is a class A felony. [1987 c 187 § 1.]

RCW 9A.32.060 Manslaughter in the first degree.

(1) A person is guilty of manslaughter in the first degree when:

(a) He recklessly causes the death of another person; or

(b) He intentionally and unlawfully kills an unborn quick child by inflicting any injury upon the mother of such child.

(2) Manslaughter in the first degree is a class A felony. [1997 c 365 § 5; 1975 1st ex.s. c 260 § 9A.32.060.]

RCW 9A.32.070 Manslaughter in the second degree.

(1) A person is guilty of manslaughter in the second degree when, with criminal negligence, he causes the death of another person.

(2) Manslaughter in the second degree is a class B felony. [1997 c 365 § 6; 1975 1st ex.s. c 260 § 9A.32.070.]

CHAPTER 8

DEBRIEFING

Immediately after defusing or restraining a subject, a debriefing should take place. You need to address who was involved, what happened, when it happened, where it happened, and why it happened. You need to take care of the injured, do an incident report, and brainstorm what went wrong and what you could have done better. The necessary personnel need to be contacted, whether it be upper management, an attorney, or law enforcement.
Everything needs to be documented in the subject's file. If it is necessary, all professionals involved with the subject need to be informed of the incident. This way others can be on alert for any similar signs of agitation.

If you anticipate criminal or civil issues, contact a private investigator to assist you in documentation, discovery of facts, background checks, pretrial preparation, surveillance, witness location, interviews, and serving subpoenas.

INJURIES

First aid needs to be provided to the subject and team members who require it. All parties need to be given the option of follow-up care. If the injured party is not of sound mind, then action should be taken to have follow-up care provided. Any injuries, along with what steps were taken for first aid, need to be well-documented.

If a person is unable to take himself to a hospital, call your local fire or police department and request assistance. Seek legal advice pertaining to assisting an injured person. In some jurisdictions, if you are certified in first aid or CPR and act in good faith, you may be protected by something called a "good samaritan law." Contact a certified instructor of first aid or CPR and take a course. The instructor will also be able to inform you if such a law exists in your area.

If you decide to transport an injured party to an emergency care facility, and if he is coherent and the injury is not life threatening, have him sign a release before doing so. When possible, have a witness verify any written, verbal, or recorded release.

ANALYSIS, NOTIFICATION, AND FOLLOW UP

Whoever is in charge—whether it be the owner, department head, supervisor, or director—should review and analyze all documentation and debriefing material. This is useful when writing policies and procedures and when training staff.

If a subject is injured, always notify your superior, the proper authorities, and the subject's family. If criminal intent was involved, I suggest that you contact law enforcement as well. If you observe the telltale signs of the subject causing harm to himself or others, and/or you have concerns about the mental health of the subject, and if it has not escalated to violence, contact a mental health professional to assess the situation. Take precautions while doing so: make sure you maintain distance, plan an escape route, and know where you're going to run for help if you need to do so.

As a courtesy, consider contacting an injured party later to see how he is doing. This is not only a personal touch but a professional one as well. How many times has a crisis developed or incident occurred that affected you emotionally? Wouldn't it have been nice if someone contacted you to see how you were? So consider doing courtesy follow-up calls.

DEBRIEFING CHECK LIST

1) Describe the incident. Where did it take place? Date & Time? Names of people involved. What do you think was the cause of the incident? Could the incident have been avoided?

2) Were all department policy guidelines followed prior to and during verbal intervention? Describe.

3) Were proper steps taken before making the decision to implement physical intervention? Describe.

4) Were all department policy guidelines followed during physical intervention? Describe.

5) Was the subject or staff injured? Describe injury. Describe how the injury happened.

6) Could the injuries have been avoided and how?

7) Were there any witnesses? Names, phone numbers or method to contact witnesses.

8) Was first aid given? To whom? Describe. Administered by whom?

9) Was the subject and/or staff offered to be taken to the hospital? If so, who took them? What hospital? What time?

10) Who was notified? Family, supervisor on duty, law enforcement, who? How were they notified? What time/date? Who made the notification? How did the notified person respond?

11) Are there any complaints against anyone? Who is the complaining person? Who is the complaint against? Describe. Witnesses to the complaint? Obtain contact phone numbers and addresses of all parties involved. Was it rectified?

12) Describe any positive interventions which the staff or team made.

13) What could the staff or team improve on?

14) Was everything documented in the case file, subject's file and were personal notes taken?

15) If necessary was photography taken of the subject's injuries, staff's injuries and scene of the incident? Was any written or recorded statements taken? If so, by whom and who has possession of them? Is there any evidence in custody? How was this evidence obtained and by whom? Who has possession of this evidence?

16) Was Law Enforcement contacted? By whom? What time? Names of officers? Case Number? What time did they arrive? While waiting for officers, describe what was taking place with the subject and staff. Were any arrests made? If so, who was arrested and where were they taken?

17) Was injured staff given an opportunity to go home? Did injured staff go home? Who took staff home? What time? When will they return to duty?

18) Was an incident report completed by the injured staff? When? Was the report completed by someone other than the injured staff? If so, whom?

19) Keep copies of everything. Give copies to all necessary personnel or chain of command.

Example of a debriefing form with typical questions and issues that need to be addressed. (Courtesy of LPI Services.)

CHAPTER 9

REAL-LIFE STORIES

The following are real-life stories involving the defusing, managing, and restraining of hostile subjects as told by professionals. They illustrate the different types of assaultive-behavior situations that professionals may face in their duties.

MENTAL HEALTH:
QUIET TIME TO VIOLENCE

A male patient in a mental health hospital, 6′2″, 230 lbs., with an assaultive history was told by staff to stop intimidating other patients. Redirection was unsuccessful, and the patient began tossing chairs and ripping books and newspapers.

He was directed to go into "quiet time," where an agitated patient is placed into an unlocked seclusion room to cool off. Patient refused and made threats to staff. Staff grouped to make a show of force. As they approached, patient clenched his fists, squatted down with legs partially bent, and said, "You better not come any closer." When one female staff got close to calm the patient down, he severely assaulted her and a male staff member who came to her aid. The patient then backed himself against the wall and wielded a chair. Staff backed off, injured staff were pulled to safety, first aid was given, and the professional assault response team was paged to respond immediately.

The response team arrived, was briefed on the situation, and a plan was developed. As team leader, I made verbal contact with the subject and attempted to misdirect and talk him down while other team members obtained a mattress for tactical purposes. The patient threw a chair at team members and then displayed an inverted metal spoon, making stabbing motions with the handle. He refused repeated verbal commands to drop the weapon and turn around.

Two team members grasped the mattress on each side and formed a pyramid formation with the rest of the team. The patient was then rammed with the mattress and pinned against the wall. While he was pinned, each of his limbs was grabbed, and two team members applied holds to the weapon hand. When the patient began to decrease his resistance, the mattress was removed and the patient was taken to the floor, where the weapon was wrestled from his hand. Leather restraints were applied and the patient was transported to a locked seclusion room. A bed was prepared with wrist, waist, and leg restraints. The patient was transferred to the bed by releasing one limb at a time and securing it; then he was medicated.

The team debriefed. There were no injuries to the team.

(Courtesy of the author, former professional assault response team coordinator.)

MENTAL HEALTH:
FEARFUL PATIENT

This situation involved a fearful patient in an adult residential treatment facility for the mentally ill. When dealing with fearful patients, staff had been trained to keep their hands open and visible, maintain a safe distance, and respond to any reasonable requests. This residential facility had a no-restraint policy, so law enforcement intervention was the only option for physical restraint. If staff was attacked, evasive defensive tactics were to be used. Resident evacuation and safety were priorities.

A mentally ill male resident, 6'0", 200 lbs., was sitting in the corner of his room with the lights out and talking to himself. The patient had a history of theft and assaultive behavior. He had just run into the facility minutes earlier and was yelling obscenities and threats to imaginary people.

Staff entered the room and began verbal intervention. The patient ordered staff in a fearful but aggressive tone of voice, "Don't come in!" Staff complied to the reasonable request and maintained a safe distance. Staff continued verbal intervention, using a calm voice and passive, nonthreatening body language. The resident was reassured that no harm was going to come to him and that staff was there to help. Resident then yelled, "Yeah, then why are the cops with you? They cannot come in!"

Believing that the resident was imagining the police presence, and in order to avoid a debate and not escalate the situation, staff informed him that the police would stand outside the door and only intervene if he became violent. Unknown to staff, the resident had shoplifted prior to running into the facility, and police were actually called by a local merchant. After they arrived and were briefed by staff, they stood in the hallway.

Rapport was eventually built between the staff and the resident. He admitted to hearing voices saying, "We're going to get you." By gaining rapport, building trust, being nonthreatening, and maintaining the "we" attitude regarding police presence, staff convinced the resident they were there to help. The resident was medicated and remained calm the rest of the evening. He was not arrested.

(Courtesy of Janet Harris, registered counselor.)

MENTAL HEALTH: LAUGHING TURNS VIOLENT

Subject was committed to a mentally ill offenders unit for second-degree assault. One day he became agitated and volatile.

Nursing staff informed me that the patient became very angry during group therapy because he felt staff and other patients were making fun of him. Staff had tried to approach the patient to calm him down, which only resulted in escalating the situation. The patient then picked up a chair and threw it through a glass partition, nearly hitting several other patients. He then went to the kitchen area, where forks and other kitchen equipment were kept. While in the kitchen he paced and talked to himself while appearing to be looking for some kind of weapon. The patient became even more agitated as staff and other patients crowded around him.

I asked all the other patients to go to their rooms or to the other side of the ward in order to give the agitated patient more space and decrease his feeling of being threatened. I then approached the patient in a calm manner and spoke to him softly, asking him what was going on. At first he would not respond. Then I asked him in a calm voice what he was feeling. He said he did not like people laughing at him and embarrassing him. I told him that I understood and would like to talk to him more about what he was feeling, but he would have to go to seclusion and calm down first.

He became somewhat less agitated when it appeared I was concerned about his feelings, but then he stated he was not going to seclusion and again became agitated. I explained to him that the staff would have security physically take him to seclusion and that would be very embarrassing for him to have everyone on the ward see this. I explained to the patient that I would personally walk him to the seclusion area and assured him no one was going to hurt him. I also told him that he would not want to give the other patients and staff the satisfaction of seeing him dragged off to seclusion. He then stated, "You're right," and asked me if I would take him to seclusion. I told him I would and that once he calmed down, I would also talk to him about why he felt so agitated.

No hospital security or show of force was needed. I was able to defuse a volatile situation by making the patient feel unthreatened,

assuring him he had my support, telling him I understood and was
concerned about his feelings, reassuring him no harm would
come to him, and explaining that he could avoid embarrassment
by not forcing hospital security to physically take him to seclusion
in front of staff and other patients.
(Courtesy of Carey Lewis, former therapy supervisor for a
secured mental offenders ward.)

CHILD PROTECTION:
STRUCK WITH SCREWDRIVER

I received a child protective service (CPS) referral of concern
regarding allegations of physical abuse. The referral stated that a
child had a quarter-size bruise on top of his forehead. The child,
age 7 years, disclosed to his teacher that his father hit him on the
forehead with the end of a screwdriver because he was angry about
the child's grades. The referral stated that the child's father was
very hostile and may have weapons in the home.

As the CPS social worker assigned to the case, I planned to use
extreme caution and requested law enforcement assistance.
Unfortunately, I was unable to get it because no police officers
were available at the time. I decided to pursue the investigation
without police assistance.

I interviewed the child at his elementary school regarding
the allegations. The child reaffirmed that his father hit him on
the forehead with a screwdriver because he was angry about his
grades. The child stated he was not afraid of his father and was
willing to go home after school. He stated it was the first time
his father had hit him and that he loved his father. He com-
mented that his father had a temper and had several weapons in
the home.

I determined the quarter-size bruise on the child's forehead
was superficial and noted that the child did not appear to be
afraid to go home, so protective custody was deemed unneces-
sary at the time. I explained to the child that I would need to

discuss the matter further with his father to ensure this kind of behavior didn't happen again. The child again informed me that his father had a bad temper and may not want to discuss anything with me.

I conducted an unannounced, early-morning home visit to discuss with the child's father the allegations of physical abuse to his son. The father was still in bed when I arrived. He became very upset when he had to get out of bed, stating he worked double shifts and was tired. I explained to him the allegations and asked him to comment. He stated the referral was not true, then became very angry and started pacing around the house. I explained that these were only allegations and that CPS is mandated by law to investigate any referrals of concern regarding possible child abuse. I said there were always two sides to every story, and that I simply wanted to hear his side.

Once the father understood that CPS was mandated by law to investigate and I was not accusing him of being a bad parent but only trying to gather information, he felt nonthreatened and began to cooperate. He explained that he had been under a lot of stress working long hours while raising a son by himself and became upset when his son brought home bad grades. He then admitted that he did lose control and, while working on his car with a screwdriver, struck his son on the forehead. He did tell his son he was sorry.

The child's father was willing to pursue anger/stress management counseling. He was also appreciative that I was not accusing or intimidating but rather understanding, willing to listen, and able to provide resources to help him deal with his problems.

(Courtesy of Carey Lewis, social worker.)

PRIVATE INVESTIGATION:
SURROUNDED BY BOUNCERS

This case evolved from an assault that resulted in a victim being punched, then cut in the neck and face with broken glass.

Witnesses were to be interviewed and subpoenas were to be served. I was hired by the attorney for the defendant.

Contact was made at a nightclub for young adults that sold alcohol and was known for violence and gang and drug activity. It had a history of police-involved incidents and drive-by shootings in the parking lot. All the bouncers wore bulletproof vests.

Attempts were made to interview management and the bouncers who were involved in breaking up the assault. Earlier attempts to interview the parties resulted in lack of cooperation and refusals to be interviewed, so subpoenas were issued.

Management became verbally abusive and hostile after being served subpoenas. Attempts to de-escalate the situation were unsuccessful. Techniques of building rapport, being sympathetic to their situation, using nonthreatening body language, and explaining that we were only trying to discover the truth were met with increased agitation.

My partner and I were relaxed and maintained a safe distance while walking toward the front door. We were then confronted by six good-sized bouncers and one manager. (It was later discovered that one of the managers was a professional kickboxer. Intelligence also revealed that the club owners were suspected of drug trafficking.)

As we exited the front door, my partner and I maintained close distance in order to protect each other's backs. Once we were outside, we handed the head bouncer a business card and asked him to contact our investigative agency. The other bouncers watched to see if their leader was going to take the card. Suddenly the manager struck my hand, slapping the card to the ground, and began to discredit the profession of private investigators, made threats of violence, and shouted obscenities. The bouncers then circled me and my partner.

We looked around to see if any objective bystanders were watching, but there was nobody other than the bouncers and manager. I knew that if I got into a fighting position, the bouncers would react violently. Instead I stood with confidence, displayed my private investigator's state license and badge, and made verbal commands: "Stop! Don't come any closer. Anybody who touches my person will be immediately arrested by the police for assault." This stopped the bouncers from coming any closer but did not stop the verbal abuse by the manager.

My partner and I slowly walked to our vehicle. Common sense should have told us to run when we were circled, but I knew that if we did it would have diminished our authoritative presence the next time we arrived.

Reestablishing control, showing confidence, speaking with authority, and giving the impression that a power greater than me was speaking through me de-escalated the situation and resulted in no violence.

(Courtesy of the author and Janet Harris, private investigators and registered process servers.)

PRIVATE INVESTIGATION:
INTERVIEW SUSPECTS OF A BURGLARY RING

My private investigative agency, LPI Services, was subcontracted by another agency to assist them in the investigation of a burglary in which money, antiques, and checkbooks had been taken.

My first objective was to interview five male suspects, one at a time and at different locations. After I interviewed the first suspect, he immediately called the others after I left his home. This became evident when I drove up to the next suspect's place of residence, where I was greeted outside by his father with, "I was expecting you. What took you so long?" He was very evasive as to the whereabouts of his son and avoided saying anything negative. I informed him that I would return the next day to speak with him.

When I arrived the next day, both of the suspect's parents were home. They kept me waiting by saying they had paged the suspect. Shortly thereafter, the suspect showed up, but he brought four other guys with him. The suspect used profanity and immediately stated that he did nothing wrong. When asked about the other guys with him, he stated they were his friends and bodyguards. The parents did nothing to calm their son down and appeared to be supporting his behavior.

As I interviewed the suspect, he became agitated and, as he escalated the situation, so did his friends. One of them stood by the door blocking my exit, another stood to my left in an aggressive stance, and the rest sat in front of me. The group appeared to be constantly looking at each other and out the front door as if waiting for a signal.

I attempted to gracefully terminate the interview, but when I did another person would start to provide information regarding the burglary. I was stuck between getting information and concerns for my safety.

I ended up defusing the situation by attempting to build rapport. I probed him for topics we had in common. I eventually discovered that they all went to the same high school and liked to work on cars. I then placed the suspect into the teacher role and myself as a student. After two hours of being educated on how to build a car engine and talking about school, I obtained good leads on the burglary case and walked away in one piece.

(Courtesy of the author, private investigator.)

PRIVATE INVESTIGATION: SURVEILLANCE AND THE .357 MAGNUM

Mel Hoover has 35 years' experience as a private investigator and is the former Washington state vice president of the American Law Enforcement Association. He is a member of the National Association of Investigative Specialists (NAIS) and is currently writing a book on real-life private investigation stories. The following is a second-hand description of a potentially violent case as related to the author by Mr. Hoover.

A prominent attorney contacted Mel with a case involving divorce and property. The attorney directed the investigator to drop everything and immediately go to the residence of his client, set up surveillance, and photograph his estranged wife as she attempted to secretly take items from the residence.

The residence was set back in a secluded area with a private driveway. The only way to get good photographs was to conduct foot surveillance down the driveway. Mel assessed the situation, analyzed the environmental conditions, and proceeded to take photos of the wife along with a group of men taking items from the residence. Suddenly one of the trucks used in taking the property drove past Mel, and the driver notified the group of his presence.

Mel was approached by the men and immediately noticed that one of them was carrying a .357 Magnum Smith & Wesson handgun. As he was confronted by the man and his cohorts, Mel immediately observed their body language, facial expressions, demeanor, and tone of voice.

Mel made verbal note of the weapon's presence to the group and attempted to keep them talking. He was able to persuade the gun wielder into putting the weapon away, keeping his eyes on the gun as it was placed into the waistband behind the the subject's back. He used a line of questioning relating to the weapon and their aggressive behavior, asking, "Is there a need to have a gun?" and, "There is no need for violence. Can we all calm down?" but he was unable to calm the group down. It was obvious that the subject's confidence and temper were escalating because of the presence of the weapon.

The gun wielder lunged at Mel's camera in an attempt to take away the evidence that he had obtained. Mel used evasive tactics to deflect the subject's attempts to grab the camera. He displayed confidence and physical ability to the group, which made them back off enough for him to obtain a safer distance. The subject then demanded the camera. Mel took a picture of the subject with the gun for additional proof of an assault.

This aggravated the subject again, and another attempt was made to assault Mel. Mel used evasive tactics once again, rendered the attack unsuccessful, assumed a safe distance, took mental notes of his assailant's physical description, and maintained a defensive posture. The group walked away while making threats and demanding that Mel leave the area at once.

Mel immediately utilized his preplanned escape route and contacted the sheriff's department, but they were on strike and did not respond. He continued with his escape plan and was able to depart the area without further incident.

Mel's ability to defuse a situation caused the subject to put the gun away. His ability to keep the group talking instead of doing helped prevent a gang attack on him. His evasive maneuvers helped prevent bodily harm and protected the evidence. Having a preplanned means of escape and leaving the scene as soon as he could saved his life. His ability to take mental documentation along with photographic proof of the event helped the attorney handle the assault and divorce cases successfully.

(Courtesy of Mel Hoover, Hoover Investigations.)

COMMUNITY CORRECTIONS OFFICER: ARRESTING SUBJECT IN CCO'S OFFICE

A community corrections officer (CCO) had called a parolee into his office for a meeting. Unknown to the subject, other CCOs were in the office waiting to arrest him for a parole violation. The subject entered and was ordered to place his hands behind his back by the lead CCO. Another CCO appeared from behind the door and attempted to cuff the subject. The subject spun in circles to avoid being cuffed, yelled profanities, and wanted to know what was going on.

The situation escalated quickly and the officers' safety became an issue. Before the situation escalated to physical attacks on the officers, the lead officer took control by using voice commands and verbal defusing techniques. The CCOs obtained a safe distance while remaining mentally ready to respond.

The lead officer commanded in a firm voice, "Stop! Listen to me! Calm down! Don't make the situation worse. Cuff up." Other commands to stop and listen were repeated, and the sub-

ject was informed that after he was cuffed he would be told what
was happening. After several more attempts to resist arrest, the
subject finally weighed out his options and chose to stop, cuff up,
and listen.

In this situation, the officer played it by the book. His training
taught him to use verbal techniques whenever dealing with a subject displaying anxiety, defensiveness, or aggressiveness or when
giving a lawful order with expectation that the subject will obey.
The CCO used verbal skills to calm and control the subject;
backed off with nonthreatening body language; used short, firm,
positive commands and a nonjudgmental tone of voice; offered a
choice; responded to the continued bad behavior; and continued
the commands until the subject was restrained.

(Courtesy of Robert Detamore, community corrections officer.)

COMMUNITY CORRECTIONS OFFICER: ARRESTING SUBJECT AT HOME

A community corrections officer organized a three-man team
to conduct an arrest at the residence of a parole violator. The plan
was to use a triangular approach—one in front and two in back.
Two vehicles were used to transport the officers to give the impression of a show of force.

The subject was working on his car as the team drove up to
the house. Before the team could get out of their vehicles, the
subject ran inside.

Each team member took up a position around the house. All
exits were blocked off, with one vehicle situated at each end of the
house. The CCOs radioed for law enforcement backup. Instead of
storming the house, which may have resulted in a lethal force situation, the officers made contact with the subject's girlfriend and
explained the options to her. She voluntarily entered the house
and convinced the subject to surrender.

The subject was arrested and cuffed without incident. In this
case the CCOs assessed the situation and utilized their resources

(the girlfriend in this case) to complete the assignment. The accurate assessment and negotiating skills of the officers made this approach successful. Their priority was the safety of themselves and the subject.

(Courtesy of Robert Detamore, community corrections officer.)

SELF DEFENSE SITUATION:
ROAD RAGE

I had made a right turn from a stop sign onto a main street. I was traveling southbound when another car driven by a young male pulled up beside me, honking his horn and yelling something. I thought there was something wrong with my car, such as a nonfunctioning tail light. I rolled down my window just as we both stopped at a traffic light. I then realized that the other driver was yelling obscenities, making threats, and accusing me of cutting him off.

My first reaction was to yell back and tell the hostile driver that I was not afraid of him. As I pondered this approach, I noticed there was another occupant in the car who also appeared to be angry.

I thought to myself, "I am trained in boxing, self-defense, and martial arts. I can beat these guys." But instead of responding with aggression, I assessed the situation. I realized that a yelling match could escalate things, and that I was outnumbered and facing an opponent in a state of rage. I considered liability and criminal issues if it were to turn physical. I also thought about the safety of all parties and how a wrong decision could effect our lives and families. These thoughts took only seconds for me to evaluate.

I decided that the appropriate thing to do was to apologize, attempt to defuse the situation, and seek safety in a well-populated area, which is what I did. The other driver noticed my nonthreatening, apologetic manner, flipped me the middle finger, and drove away. So did I.

Today I wonder what would have happened if I had gotten angry when the driver flipped me off. Someone else might have responded with their own middle finger and started the aggressive encounter all over again. To drive away was the right decision.

Remember, when you have defused the situation, don't aggravate the other person all over again. Self-defense is the art of fighting without fighting.

(Courtesy of the author.)

TRANSIT BUS OPERATOR:
GANG TROUBLE ON THE BUS

There are many types of gangs that operate in the city, including Samoan, Vietnamese, black, white, and Hispanic gangs. The two main gangs in our city are the Crips and the Bloods. They thrive on intimidation and violence. On several occasions we have had shootings on the bus. The bus company provided training for us, but the best training I've had came from Ed Lewis. The following is how I used his training.

While driving my route, I observed a group of gang members causing trouble in the rear of the bus. They were using profanity, making playful threats against one another, and flashing gang signs. You could feel the anger and hostility within the group. They acted as if they owned the bus and appeared to have no respect for the rights of other passengers. Their demeanor displayed the arrogance of being untouchable.

Usually there is one leader who motivates the others, so I watched and waited for this individual to reveal himself through body language and other signs. Once I discovered who the leader was, I thought about what type of communication should be used. I had the option of using the PA system or attempting a one-to-one approach.

I quickly determined that using the PA system would not be the best method. My experience warned me that using it could end up in a confrontation. I was afraid that the group would feel embarrassed or disrespected if I started yelling over the PA, or that the leader might take it as a threat to his power and status within the gang. I did not want to provoke an already dangerous situation, so I decided to call the leader to the front of the bus. This decreased the chance that I could be gang attacked.

As I built rapport with the leader, I slowly explained to him the rules of the bus. I tried not to talk to him in a confrontational manner, and I tried to use slang so he could see that I identified with him. During this intervention, it seemed as if time stood still. It was a very intense moment.

He and I had a meeting of minds. He went back to his seat feeling that I gave him respect. In return, he respected the rules of the bus.

The rapport I developed with this young man continues today. He no longer causes trouble.

(Courtesy of Darryl Briggs, transit bus operator.)

REFERENCES

Edward Lewis has studied and trained with some of the top martial artists, private investigators, and physical restraint professionals in the world. This book is a compilation of his experience, training, and education. The following are the organizations, occupations, and other resources from where he gained his knowledge and experience:

Occupations and Positions

Caseworker, Washington State Child Protective Services
Family reconciliation services for dysfunctional families
Group life counselor, Boys Ranch for Juvenile Offenders
Mental health tech, Western State Mental Hospital
Participant, community programs for at-risk youth
Private case management services for mentally ill veterans of war
Regional representative, International Sports Karate Association (ISKA)
Regional representative, Karate International Council of Kickboxing (KICK)
Regional representative, Professional Karate Association (PKA)
Registered counselor, state of Washington

Registered process server, state of Washington
Self-defense instructor, Tacoma Chapter of the Guardian Angels
South Hall coordinator, Dr. Armstrong Professional Assault Team

Courses
Anger management and domestic violence classes
Boxing program—Eastside Boys and Girls Club
Private investigation course, ICS
Private investigation course, William C. Dear & Associates
Private investigation and certified training course,
   Linda Montgomery Investigations
Professional assault response training
Psychology, sociology, and communication classes
S.A.F.E. and Protecting Angel programs
Violence prevention programs
William Ruddell International, Washington State Investigative
Licensing Laws

Organizations and Schools
American Lake Veteran's Hospital, Continuing Education
Association of Christian Investigators (ACI)
National Association of Investigative Specialists (NAIS)
Pacific Lutheran University
Washington Association of Legal Investigators (WALI)

Individuals
Robin Aguillion, judo and jiu jitsu
Master Steve Armstrong, Isshin-ryu karate
Darryl Briggs, transit bus driver
Master Chui Brocka, Ernesto Presas, and Professor Remy Presas,
   Philippine martial arts/arnis
Robert Detamore, community corrections officer
Don Gulla, police officer
Janet Harris, private investigator and registered counselor
Carey Lewis, social worker, former therapy supervisor
   for mentally ill offenders unit

Ralph Thomas, NAIS
Sifu Roger Tung and Sifu Steve Thommen, kung fu instructors
Bill Wallace, Joe Lewis, Victor Solier, and Kathy Long,
    kickboxing champions
Discussions with caseworkers, social workers, psychologists,
    psychiatrists, and public servants

Books and References

American Heritage Dictionary of the English Language
Art of Surveillance by Kelly Riddle
Barron's Law Dictionary, 3rd Edition
Close Encounters by Takayuki Kubota
Diagnostic and Statistical Manual of Mental Disorders,
    4th Edition
Dorland's Illustrated Medical Dictionary, 27th Edition
The Pretext Book by Roy Slade and James Gutzs
Private Investigations Made Easy by Kelly Riddle
Revised Code of Washington (RCW)
The Tao of Jeet Kune Do by Bruce Lee

NOTE: None of the agencies, schools, professionals, authors, publishers, individuals, associations, organizations, their agents, or their associates have endorsed or implied endorsement of this book.

ABOUT THE AUTHOR

Edward Lewis, a graduate of Pacific Lutheran University, where he majored in communications, has taught self-defense courses since 1967. He has been listed in *Who's Who In Karate* and is a former regional representative for the Karate International Council of Kickboxing and PKA Full Contact Karate. Lewis has taught the Guardian Angels, a community crime watch organization, and has created violence prevention programs for law enforcement and social service professionals, specifically for at-risk youths with gang potential. He has appeared as a guest speaker on KWJZ, a Seattle-based radio station, and has spoken about violence prevention and missing children at the Safe Street National Night Out Violence Prevention Fair. He has been affiliated with the National Center for Missing and Exploited Children.

Lewis is the former South Hall coordinator of the Dr. Armstrong Team for Western State Mental Hospital. Dr. Armstrong is an elite team that defuses, restrains, and gains control of assaultive mentally ill patients. Registered with the state of Washington as a mental health counselor, he served as co-therapist in an anger management group at Western State Hospital and helped juvenile offenders manage undesirable behavior. Lewis has served as a field case manager for mentally ill veterans of war, many of whom had a history of unpredictable violent episodes. He is certified in Professional Assault Response Training by Western State Hospital.

Lewis is the founder of the Protecting Angel/S.A.F.E. Program covering a wide range of self-defense and crime prevention topics for professionals, families, and at-risk youths.

Lewis is currently the owner and operator of a private investigative agency and a registered state process server. He is a member of the Washington Association of Legal Investigators, National Association of Investigative Specialists, and Association of Christian Investigators.

For speaking engagements, seminars, workshops, or private investigative services, visit his Web site (address below) or contact him directly in care of the publisher.

http://www.angelfire.com/biz/lpiserve/

If you liked this book, you will also want to read these:

RESTRAINT AND CONTROL FOR SECURITY INDUSTRY PROFESSIONALS (Video)
With Gary Fliegner
Learn everything you need to know to effectively control unruly subjects while keeping yourself safe. Security expert Gary Fliegner reveals the secrets of both the techniques and the tactics of the professional security trade and shows you how to make an exciting living while staying alive. Color, approx. 60 min.
#10011393

REAL WORLD SELF-DEFENSE
A Guide to Staying Alive in Dangerous Times
by Jerry VanCook
This entertaining book offers savvy advice for dealing with everything from a violent attack to the often ironic legal aftermath. VanCook, a former undercover cop, has experienced the realities of street violence *and* the legal system. His simple approach to self-defense stresses mind-set and covers armed and unarmed tactics and techniques. 5 1/2 x 8 1/2, softcover, photos, 224 pp. **#10010809**

SAFE IN THE CITY
A Streetwise Guide to Avoid Being Robbed, Raped, Ripped Off, or Run Over
by Marc "Animal" MacYoung and Chris Pfouts
This is an entertaining street-level look at how crimes are really committed in America's cities. Chris and Animal use their NY–L.A. experience to help you learn the games carjackers, muggers, "gangstas," rapists, junkies and conmen play—and how to avoid them. 5 1/2 x 8 1/2, softcover, 320 pp. **#10004372**

A PROFESSIONAL'S GUIDE TO ENDING VIOLENCE QUICKLY
How Bouncers, Bodyguards, and Other Security Professionals Handle Ugly Situations
by Marc "Animal" MacYoung
People who deal with violence on a daily basis know that the best way to avoid getting injured or sued by the jerk who started the trouble is to defuse the situation or put him down fast and hard. Here Animal shows you how to do both. 5 1/2 x 8 1/2, softcover, illus., 256 pp. **#10005296**

STREET SMARTS, FIREARMS, AND PERSONAL SECURITY
Jim Grover's Guide to Staying Alive and Avoiding Crime in the Real World
Here are the best of Jim Grover's "Personal Security" columns in *Guns & Ammo* covering the entire spectrum of crime avoidance and defense. Includes gaining street savvy, hardening your home, traveling safely, utilizing armed and unarmed options and training for practical firearm use. 8 1/2 x 11, softcover, photos, illus., 280 pp. **#10011328**